Drink and Damnation
A light-hearted look at Leicester's Drinking Dens

By Barry Lount & Robert Spurr

Despite Hitler's best efforts, Barry Lount was not injured during the bombing of his former employer's premises. Allegedly, a report of this air raid was intercepted and later decoded by the team at Bletchley Park, was roughly translated to: 'missed the bugger'!

Produced by Steamin' Billy Brewing Co. Ltd. 2012

Drink and Damnation

A light-hearted look at Leicester's Drinking Dens

Produced by Steamin' Billy Brewing Co. Ltd. 2012

ISBN: 978-1-907540-72-1

Published November 2012

Printed and Published by Anchorprint Group Limited
www.anchorprint.co.uk

Table of contents

Author's Note

Most of these stories were sourced, over a long period of time, from contemporary records, newspaper articles and court reports, as well as a diversity of lesser known previously published material.

Local residents - many sadly no longer with us - proved a rich source of personal reminiscence.

Some of these stories relate humorous events. However, many are a reflection of the extreme hardship and poverty endured by the ordinary man and woman. Their stories are candidly observed. It would be wrong to judge their lives by today's standards.

1

Bawdy Taverns

Taverns and alehouses have always been associated with bawdy tales.

Upon their accession to the British throne in 1689, William and Mary of Orange introduced to their adopted country a relatively unknown and exiting new drink – Gin. A general acceptance and enthusiasm for this newest form of alcohol meant that people could brew and sell this spirit without hindrance of any Government taxation. Thus, private dwelling houses quickly became distilleries and respectable front parlours dens of iniquity! This drink, brewed from good English grain and flavoured with juniper berries was both cheap and easy to make and, very soon, towns and villages across the country were indulging in the making and consumption of this most potent of liquors.

The satirical artist, William Hogarth (1697-1764) famously depicted the resulting mayhem:

William Hogarth's 'Gin Lane'

A writer of the time reported:

'A trader has a large empty room, where his wretched guests get intoxicated, they are laid together in heaps, promiscuously, men, women and children, till they recover their senses, when they proceed to drink on'.

One alarming incident in 1736 tells of:

'One Fossett a cobbler, and a person by the name of Joss the glazier, Summers a bricklayer, Roy a carman (a carrier) and one or two others, met accidentally at a gin shop. They drank gin in half pint glasses without intermission, to so great an excess that Joss the glazier fell backwards with the eleventh half pint in his hand and died on the spot, about eight o'clock at night. Summers died in the same shop at about three o'clock in the morning. The others by advice of Mr Lee a surgeon, had oil and warm water poured down their throats, which set them vomiting, though one is said to be dead since. Roy was sent to the parish nurse and remained there speechless for ten days'.

Sometimes, the alewife would offer sexual favours to customers.

On Fair Days, anyone had the right to brew and sell their own ale without any form of licence, which drew the comment; *'abandoned females are entertained in temporary beer houses and suffered to molest every person who passes them and seduce the unwary in the face of day.'*

The Jolly Miller

Leicester certainly had its' dens of iniquity. The Jolly Miller, an ancient thatched Inn on Granby Street, was known in 1751 as a 'gin shop'. It stood seven or eight yards back from the pavement, on a lower level than the road. It was approached down a set of steps in front of which grew four large trees and the pub's sign hung in one of the trees. It displayed a colourful painting of a jolly man in miller's attire with a rubicund face, holding a foaming quart of ale in one hand and a long pipe in the other. It was situated on, or close to, the original site of Leicester's original cock-pit.

The Jolly Miller eventually became The Falcon, but was later closed due to 'certain irregularities'. It was, in fact, a known as a venue for thieves and ne'er-do-wells and had its' licence revoked in 1873 as it was said to have been the habitual resort of prostitutes.

After The Falcon ceased trading as a public house it continued, for a period, as the headquarters of the All Saints Brewery. Thomas Godfrey Cock resided there with his wife and her two sisters, later to be joined by his father who had also been engaged in brewing. The advertisement illustrated above dates from 1879 and shows the Granby Street premises as the central offices for the All Saints Brewery.

The Turkey Cafe

The Turkey Café, designed by Arthur Wakerley for J.S. Winn & Company and featuring Art Nouveau tiles, was built on the Granby Street site in 1900-01. This stylish edifice is an outstanding architectural structure and justifiably a listed building. William Neatby of the London based establishment Doulton & Company designed the tiles. Neatby also designed the tiles for the façade of the Harrods Meat Hall and the Blackpool Winter Gardens.

A similar style of public house, called The Fox and Anchor, also displaying Neatby's tiles stands today on Charterhouse Street in the City of London, close by Smithfield's meat market. Rather than turkeys displaying and strutting their stuff, the detail of the Fox and Anchor tiles feature peacocks. If any copying of design was involved happily the Turkey Café just pre-dates the other building!

The Fox and Anchor, London.

The Turkey Café, Leicester

In 1897 Winn's 'offers' included a smoke room special, consisting of a cup of delicious coffee with cream and a cigarette, all for a set price of 2d. It took a further 75 years before a licence to sell alcohol was granted 1955 and, even then, the licence stated that alcohol could only be sold at certain times, during the afternoon tea dances! The Turkey Café today is now fully licensed and retains its' popularity.

The Magpie

The Magpie was an apt name for a public house that was the habitual resort of thieves.

First recorded in 1600, a narrow passageway ran from the old building in Gallowtree Gate through to the market place. The front elevation of the building was white-washed and had six lead casement windows, with chequers painted on the window shutters, together with the words: 'Rum, Shrub & Purl sold here.' Purl was a mixture of ale, gin and herbs, usually ginger; it was normally served hot as a pick-me-up, so long as you did not pick up too many! Shrub was a mixture of citrus fruits, normally lemon or orange mixed with sugar and rum; other spirits could be used depending on your taste.

A hanging sign proudly portrayed The Magpie. Although it was later to change its' name to the Crown & Magpie in the late 18th century, it never quite lost its reputation for dubious clientele.

Francis 'Tanky' Smith

'Tanky' Smith, the famous Leicester detective, would often make the Magpie his first port of call when investigating crimes. Tanky was a member of Leicester's newly augmented police force (founded in 1836) to help rid Leicester of its crime-ridden streets. In 1840 the force established the new rank of detective and Tanky was appointed as one of two new officers holding that position.

In 1864 he became a private detective and in a similar way to Sir Arthur Conan Doyle's character, Sherlock Homes, Tanky employed the use of disguises in tracking down criminals. The building known as Top Hat Terrace on the London Road depict sixteen carved heads, all illustrating the different disguises that he used. The property was built with the reward money Tanky had received through catching criminals and was designed by his son who was an architect. It remains a pleasing though quirky addition to Leicester's architecture. Built with the proceeds indirectly connected to crime, it bears testament to the fact that crime can pay and is a reminder that Victorian Leicester was a consistently lawless town. Ironically, the majority of the building's present occupants are solicitors!

Coffee Houses

The introduction of coffee into the country saw the launch of fashionable coffee houses. Based on taverns, though attempting to display higher standards and attract a different type of clientele, they provided smoking rooms and sold wine and beer alongside coffee and tea and were bound by the same licensing principles. In contrast, some were little more than alehouses adapting to a new vogue. For example, the Saracen's Head became the Saracen's Head Coffee House, the Bear and Swan was renamed the Bear and Swan Coffee House. No expense was involved in re-branding in those days, "just paint 'and coffee house' on the sign Fred!"

A Coffee House smoking room.

Magistrates, informed of the disorderly nature of some of the coffee houses, reported: *"There are places in Leicester called Coffee Houses which are regular dens of infamy. On Sunday morning, there were 13 dogs during daytime service, children of both sexes enticed to the place, and allowed to smoke, drink and game."*

Eventually coffee shops became more refined, less, many dropping the sale of alcohol completely and succumbing to the Temperance ideal. They were often also known as Coffee Taverns.

The three most eminent sites standing as a reminder of the former grand coffee houses were the rebuilt 1880's High Cross Coffee House on the corner of High Street and Highcross Street, now a Wetherspoons pub, The East Gates Coffee House (1885) on the corner of Churchgate, and the Victoria on Granby Street. All were owned by the aptly named Leicester Coffee and Cocoa House Company, founded in 1877. It is still possible to stand outside the Victoria Coffee House and imagine a time when a pork pie could be purchased for 3d., and a glass of 'Hop Ale' for 1½d., in the Ladies First Class Refreshment Room! Of the twelve coffee houses in Leicester, ten followed a standard design but the two commissioned by The Leicester Coffee and Cocoa House Company, which were East Gates and the Victoria (built in 1887-88), were clearly regarded as 'First Class' and the design concept was entrusted to the extremely talented local architect Edward Burgess.

The elegant Victoria Coffee House (designed by Edward Burgess) Granby Street circa 1897, with the Wellington public house next door, now a Tesco store. Although open long hours, the modern-day shop would not have competed with the Coffee House, whose opening hours began at 5 a.m. with coffee and/or tea and coffee costing just one penny a pint!

The East Gates coffee house.

The Welford Coffee House (circa 1890) on the corner of Welford Road and Marlborough Street.

The Crown and Cushion

Leicester had two Crown & Cushion pubs; one at 75 Belgrave Gate, the other at 32 Churchgate, both harbouring low life and prostitutes. The Crown & Cushion in Belgrave Gate, previously called The Cannon in 1720, had its' landlord fined during the 1880's many times for letting his house be used for prostitution. Further landlords failed to heed the warning they, too, were fined for the same offence. Eventually, the pub lost its licence two days before Christmas in 1914.

You really could not make this up and be believed, following the closer of the Falcon, owned by Thomas Cock, for allowing prostitution on the premises the landlord of the Crown & Cushion, who turned a blind eye to the offence, was named Hoare!

THE CROWN AND CUSHION.

With regard to the Crown and Cushion, the tenant of which is Frederick Charles Hoare, and the owners Robinson's Brewery, Ltd., Inspector North, giving evidence in support of the objection to renewal, said there were five other licensed houses in close proximity. The house was frequented by low class customers, and the time had undoubtedly arrived when the house ought to be closed.

Mr. Wm. Simpson, who appeared for the owners, said he could not deny that this particular district was overcrowded with licensed houses. The license was referred for compensation.

The closure of the Crown & Cushion Belgrave Gate

The Crown & Cushion in Churchgate suffered the same fate, when it lost its licence in 1897, after Alfred Brown the licensee appeared court four times, once for permitting drunkenness and three times for allowing prostitutes to ply their trade there. His licence was finally revoked for permitting his pub to be used as a brothel.

In the 1950s and early 60s women who made a living from prostitution would in addition procure their clients from the cafes situated around the City centre. These included Horner's Dining Rooms at 22. Churchgate. Most people knew it as Horner's café and it according to some people it had a dubious reputation.

Standing on the corner of Humberstone Gate was a converted single-decker bus, painted blue and with a high counter. This make shift enterprise was called The Wagon hot dog and drinks stand, operated by a man called Don. It became one of places used by such ladies of the street as Bella who was very well known in the area. She was once described as being "a bit stout, but good at it". who would also frequenting the hot dog stand was Eskimo Lill, well built, and wearing a coat with a fur collar she did indeed look like an Eskimo. Also refreshing herself at The Wagon was Margot, a very attractive lady, who moved to London where "she a made lot of money." Following an altercation in 1954, a local man stabbed one of the women with a penknife fatally wounding her. The incident, which took place just around the corner from the hot dog stand in the Vestry Street yard, made headlines at the time. Other well-known prostitutes were Molly, Doll, Iris, and 'red boot Rosie', who frequented the Charnwood Street area.

Another tavern to enter this 'hall of fame' as a house of ill repute was The Opera House built circa 1685 in Guildhall Lane. Originally the Queens or Maidens Head, it changed its name to the Opera House around the time of the 20th century. Standing In the shadow of Leicester Cathedral, it caused a stir when its owners were prosecuted for allowing gaming and prostitution to take place on the premises. The top floor even had a trap door through which 'interested' customers could secretly watch cavorting couples in the room below. Found guilty of running it as a brothel it, the owner lost his licence in 1913. It reopened as The Opera House restaurant in around 2003 and as a bar in 2007.

Victorian Leicester delighted in the organised entertainments held in its pubs. Indeed one could say they were the fore runners to the music halls. Public houses held their own 'free and easy' evenings. In some cases (and much to the disgust of the Temperance Movement) these bawdy sing- a-longs would acquire publicity in the press. Sam Torr of the Green man was a major player in the promotion of such musical delights.

SPECIAL NOTICE.

MARTIN HOGAN,

Pianist and Tenor Vocalist, (late of Sam Hague's Minstrels, is engaged at the

CHAMPION, *HUMBERSTONE GATE,*

AND WILL APPEAR EVERY EVENING.

N.B. The only place of the kind in Leicester where you can hear legitimate talent.

Proprietor,—C. Woodford.

This advert is from the 1880s.
Martin Hogan was a former member of Sam Hague's slave troupe of Georgia Minstrels.
Not un-surprisingly, the Temperance Movement, took strong exception to this kind of entertainment.

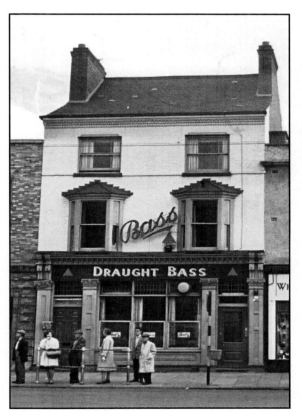

The Champion pub (pictured) became the target of 'The Blue Ribbon Army'. The drunkard in the barrel represents an inebriated customer berating William Booth, the moral crusader. The Champion had a strong Irish connection. It was used in the 1950s and 60s by construction workers and Humberstone Gate was the main collection point for the majority of Leicester's Irish building workers. The pub was always a lively place for a bevy. It was renamed in the 1970s as the Hansome Cab.

In the 1850s Mary Jones, alias Poll Jones and Poll Doyle, ran a house of ill repute in Orchard Street. She combined her business with theft, pick pocketing and burglary, in fact, any kind of crime that came her way.

Mary Jones, together with George Loydall with whom she had a tempestuous relationship worked a number of scams. Jones was adept at pick pocketing and robbing her clients whilst they were engaged in amorous pursuits. Men who had been relieved of their money and valuables whilst engaged in sexual activities frequently contacted the Police. Mary, Loydall, and other accomplices graduated to street robbery and this came to light when one Amos Toone reported to the police that he had been dispossessed of his watch and money behind the Bower Inn on Coventry Street. Somehow, his story didn't quite ring true and during police questioning Toone admitted he had concocted the story to cover his embarrassment.

It transpired that Toone, after a few drinks at the Bower, had been making his way into town along St Nicholas Street. On the corner of Jewry Wall Street he was propositioned by Mary Jones, who he accompanied to a nearby passage way, and allowed her to *'make free with him'* - unlikely to be free, but you get the gist! Two men, one of whom claimed to be her husband, then disturbed the couple. The two men held Toone down while Mary ran off, followed shortly by her two accomplices. Toone was left pulling up his trousers and wondering where his money went. The local newspaper described it as *'a daring grotto robbery committed in Leicester.'*

The Bower Inn taken shortly before demolition.

Dancing in the wrong room

The De Montfort in Wellington Street was once regarded as a respectable pub, one of the few houses in Leicester to sell Barnsley bitter. In the early 1990s it became a haven for drug dealing and was subsequently closed down in 1993. It then reopened renamed as the Wig and Pen reflecting the nearby law courts.

A less serious incident took place in 1955 when the licensee was cautioned for allowing people to *'dance in the lounge'* in contravention of his music and singing license.

The Friar Tuck

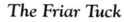

Another to have its license revoked and closed down was the Friar Tuck Woodgate after many run ins and reports of *'goings on'* a spokesperson from the city's licensing committee reported that they were to intimidated to enter and check it out. The pub finally had its license taken away in 2007 after two men were shot and a further two were stabbed in the pub.

The Eclipse

The Eclipse was named after the legendary racehorse of the same name. In 1946 the landlord was fined for 5 offences of watering the beer down, wisely he left shortly afterwards.

The Eclipse was another pub that was frequented by 'ladies of the night' and even today if you mention its name to older Leicester people you are usually met by a wry smile,

Bawdy taverns had virtually died out by the seventies, a few still existed around the clock tower with a 'reputation' none more so than the Eclipse in Eastgates it was one that Barry's father warned him not to go in, so being a teenager he did just the opposite.

'A pint of mild please' he ordered at the bar, the pint was duly pulled and placed on the bar in front of him a hand came from over his shoulder and picked up the pint. Barry turned and gazed open mouthed as the stranger sank the pint in one. 'Thanks son' the man muttered and gave him a menacing stare, Barry paid for the pint and slunk off to the corner with his companion without saying a word. Before he left a scuffle broke out and someone was carried out of the front door. That was his introduction to the Eclipse.

Robert Spurr had a slightly different experience in there, aged about seventeen (none of this over 25 I.D. nonsense in those days, if you were big enough and earned some money you could always get a pint) he was a regular at the Churchill, later Winston's and now known as The Lamp Lighters. On his way to that pub he passed the Eclipse. His over riding memory of the place was that the front window always seemed to be either smashed, or under repair. For similar reasons to Barry he went in there for a pint, managed to drink it successfully (all be it hiding in the rear of the bar) and escaped unharmed.

2
Eat, drink and be merry, politics and corruption

Prior to the electoral reforms the Council was run by the Tory party, they were not elected they just appointed themselves. The Alderman appointed the Councillors, when an Alderman died a senior Councillor was chosen. The Aldermen then picked another Tory party supporter to join the Common Council as a replacement. It was extremely corrupt and they strongly believed in looking after own interests. Land was sold cheaply to fellow Council members; loans and contracts were awarded to party members. Most people in the licensed trade were staunch Tory supporters and they often held influential civic posts. Some of the pubs ran by Tory Council members included these. Councillor Oliver owned the Unicorn, Alderman Johnson the Bull and Alderman Gregory the Black Lion. Aldermen and Council members Birkley, Watts, Peach, and Forester were all brewers and publicans. Alderman Newton was the landlord of the Horse and Trumpet. He was married three times to wealthy wives and after they had all died he was able to retire as a publican and live the life of a gentleman. (Seems strange to lose three rich wives, however he was probably in safe hands as the coroner was also a fellow Councilman).

In 1814 the Three Crowns was ran by William Bishop, it was previously owned by his father James Bishop (Bishop Street is named after him) both men were Council members, Aldermen and held office as Mayor. It was the preferred Inn for all the Council functions around this period. It is commonly stated that the Three Crowns was built about 1726 and named this to mark the union of the 3 crowns of Hanover, England and Scotland on the accession of George 1st in 1714. However an article written in 1880 states that it was named the Three Crowns long before this to celebrate the arrival of James 1st in England, and the Three Crowns were those of Scotland, Ireland and England. It also says that it was a popular Inn for travellers at the time of the great plague in 1669. The building appeared externally to be early Georgian but it could well have been a replacement or a redevelopment of an earlier building.

The Council held their Venison feast there in August 1745 and it was ordered that a hogshead of ale, or more, if Mr Mayor shall think fit, be drank at the charge of the Corporation. The article goes on to say *"And most probably Mr Mayor did think fit, for the accounts show that the Leicester Burgesses were jolly dogs and drank the bottle deep in those days"*. A hogshead is a 54 gallon barrel, that's 432 pints not bad for starters.

The last coach journey from the Three Crowns circa 1868, the advent of the railways drove a nail into the Inns coffin. About two years later the hotel was demolished.

Each year the appointed Mayor was given a pipe of wine, it appears to have been largely for his own use as one year the Mayor received a payment of about £100 in lieu of his barrel of wine .A pipe was a barrel, which held 108 gallons, 864 pints. That's about two and a half-pints seven days a week for the year, small wonder you only served one year in office! It also seems amazing that at virtually all the Council feasts and functions it was at Mr Mayors discretion as to how much wine and ale he should think fit to be consumed on the occasion. Given that he may have already had a pint or two of his wine allocation he was probably in no fit state to decide anything!

Did you know?

In the reign of Henry 8th the daily diet allowed for a lady of the bed chamber by royal warrant, included a gallon of ale at breakfast, another at dinner, half a gallon of ale with a manchet (fine quality wheat bread, loaf or roll) in the afternoon. Followed by a gallon of ale and half a gallon of wine at supper!

Political Bribery is certainly not new and if anything may have at times been more transparent. At the election for Parliament in 1754 Tory's George Wright and James Wigley noted in their electoral expenses that a total of £3,104.11s.4d was spent on drinks and money paid individually for votes bought.

Inns were visited and were on occasions paid to display 'the colours' with each Inn allowed an amount to bribe voters with drink, those without the franchise to vote were given drink to wear 'the colours'

Itemised accounts ranged from 1s.1d spent on drink at the modest Tailors Arms in Chatham Street to £125 at the Dolphin, £180 at the Three Crowns and a massive £323 at the upmarket Three Cranes. Three hundred Colliers were imported from Coleorton and armed with bludgeons with spikes inserted in them. They were employed 'just to help' along the Tory cause, George Wright and James Wigley were duly elected.

As only freemen had the right to vote, it was the less well off of them that were targeted for bribes of free ale and refreshments in the period leading up to the election. Some of these had become freemen due to their service in a trade or by inheritance and they took full advantage of their status by accepting as much free hospitality as possible. It does make you consider if the term 'floating voter' owes its origin from this time! Some of the public houses even paid a 'retainer' in return for them being chosen as one of the selected establishments where voters could be supplied with drinks.

In the election of 1826 it was estimated to have cost in the region of £50,000 to get the two Tory candidates elected to parliament. The Council had written to 2,000 people offering them free status as freemen of the Borough in return for their vote for the 'blue' candidates. About 800 took up this offer, 14 of which were Baronets, 104 Clergymen, none of who lived in or had any real connection with Leicester. This caused the Council to sink deeply into debt and the ensuing arguments, claims and counter claims about how much the candidates should pay towards these costs became public. It so badly damaged the reputation of the Council that it took many years to repair. One of the elected candidates was Robert Otway Cave, who turned out not to be a very 'true blue' candidate after all. Some Tory candidates were by this time becoming more left wing and became supporters of reform. Otway Cave later went on to be a M.P. for Hastings and his home Town of Tipperary until his death in November 1844.

It was stated that the election of 1826 had culminated in two weeks of drunken fighting, for candidates who had little interest in the town, decided by many voters who had no interest at all in the town. All this ultimately resulted in a legal enquiry into the accounts and practices of the Council.

For many years only freemen were allowed to sell ales and spirits in Leicester. A payment of about £50 was required to become a freeman and this would be granted by the Town Council. In this way they would regulate who could set up in business and get a licence. With their strong political bias they made sure that only Tory voters met the criteria. When the Beer Act was passed in 1830 they successfully appealed against it being adopted in Leicester as it might deprive the freemen of Leicester this sole right to sell ale. Some beer houses did open but many were outlets for the established Tory brewers. Things changed dramatically when the Whigs won the municipal elections after the reforms of 1835 and many more beer houses soon became established.

> **TUESDAY, JUNE 4.**
> *(Sittings in Banco.)*
> THE CORPORATION OF LEICESTER V. BURGESS.
> The question in this case arose upon the construction of the late Beer Act. It appeared that the freemen of Leicester were exclusively entitled by custom to retail beer, ale, &c., and the point in dispute was, whether under the new Beer Act licences could be granted to persons not so entitled.
> The COURT, after hearing at length the arguments of the Solicitor-General and Mr. Amos this day, decided that the act, although intended to increase the facility of granting licences, did not extend to deprive the freemen of Leicester of their peculiar privileges, and that non-freemen of that place were not entitled to licences.

A report from The Times newspaper in 1832. The Tory Council members would go to great lengths to look after their own interests. This 'custom' was one purely created by themselves and effectively quashed any competition.

> ### *Did you know?*
> It was not uncommon for the Corporation to provide the preacher at St Martin's Church with a gallon of wine after the Sunday morning service to "comfort his inner man"!

Thomas the troubled Town Clerk

Thomas Burbidge aged 29 an attorney of law and a gentleman was appointed as the Town Clerk on the 20th of September 1813, following the resignation of William Heyrick.

Thomas's father Joseph started in business as a brush maker in Belgrave Gate, he had eight children with his first wife Rebecca, who died at the age of 29. He then married Mary Palmer with whom he fathered another five children, the eldest son being Thomas, born on the 1st of April 1784. Joseph became a member of the Town Council from 1774. He was appointed as an Alderman in 1789 a post he held until his death in September of 1807 aged 58. He was additionally a Justice of the Peace during the years of 1792-96 and was appointed Mayor in 1792.

Framework knitting was the main industry for Leicester men; many were in distress and had to revert to Parish relief. By 1815 the frame workers again saw their wages fall, unrest was in the air The Hampden Club was set up in many towns to further aims of political liberty and the franchise to vote. The Anchor was the appointed meeting place but so great were the numbers attending that some were obliged to gather at The Bowling Green Inn.

The Corporation was much disturbed by these events so the Town Clerk Thomas Burbidge wrote to the Home Secretary for him to curb the meetings by giving the corporation increased powers. He replied asking Burbidge for evidence and to keep surveillance on the meetings, Burbidge engaged a spy to conceal himself in a barrel at The Bowling Green and listen in.

The Town Clerk was paid an annual basic salary of two hundred pounds this was increased greatly by being paid for any additional services he performed. Thomas also took on many other Council duties some were by appointment and others he simply adopted. These included being the Receiver for the Alderman Newton Estates, Steward of the Borough, Under Bailiff, Assessor to the Coroner, Clerk to the Magistrates and Clerk to the Visitors of the Lunatic Asylum.

In 1834 the Council accounts list the following payments made to Thomas in addition to his basic salary mentioned earlier:

£100   *was paid to him as Steward of the Borough.*

£397 and £164   *for bills relating to business regarding the Electoral Reform Act.*

£251   *for journeys to London relating to returns required by the House of Commons about the Sir Thomas White charity trust.*

£141   *for other journeys to London.*

£518   *for two bills again relating to the Reform Act and the Commissioners Enquiry.*

£328   *for an action against a beer house keeper and a further bill relating to the Reform Act.*

Thomas during his period in office misappropriated funds from the Sir Thomas White charity, the Wyggeston hospital and others He had also sold land to himself at advantageous prices. When he was dismissed many thought he was extremely lucky not to be charged with criminal offences. Thomas ignored these accusations and claimed between £12,000 & £20,000 in loss of earnings as compensation from the Corporation.

The Whigs took on a large debt from the old Corporation in 1836 amounting to £30,564 with an additional £ 7,250 owed by Thomas Burbidge to Sir Thomas White's charity. The Court of Chancery decided that the Council had to repay Burbidge`s debt.

Thomas's compensation claim was eventually settled in 1853 they agreed to pay him a lump sum of £400 with an additional £200 in the first year, and £600 a year for the rest of his life. Fortunately for the ratepayers he died two years later in a debtor's jail where his wine merchants (for failure to pay his debts) had consigned him.

3
Riots & Rough - Houses

Throughout history Leicester folk have enjoyed a good old riot, from the Chartists to cheese riots, framework knitters to factory fracas. These have often occurred in or around alehouses and Taverns.

The cheese riots in Leicester occurred when prior to the cheese fair of 1766 a mob incensed by the increasing price of cheese, set about the cheese sellers believing them to be profiteering. Wagons of cheese were looted and the cheese warehouse at the Bell Hotel was ransacked, before some semblance of calm was instilled when the guard was called out and the remaining cheeses were taken to the Old Exchange in the Market Place they were placed under protection there before being put on sale the next day.

The Old Exchange building 1748-1851

Circa 1900 the cheese market outside the later Corn Exchange building. Health and food safety was obviously not an issue in those days, just lay it in on some straw on the ground and hopefully ward off any 'passing' dog who may want to relive itself!

The Poor Law riots of 1848, occurred when the unemployed were forced to work in the stone yards for inadequate pay. Riots ensued for days and nights culminating in police breaking down doors in Wharf Street and indiscriminately attacking anyone inside, after it must be said, that the police themselves had been stoned from some of the houses. Incensed by this the mob attacked the Yeomanry stationed at the Bell Hotel eventually being repelled and forced back down Wharf Street by large reinforcements of police and troops.

The Fleur-de-lis in Belgrave Gate was also known as a radical house, as was the Anchor on the corner of Charles and Halford Street along with the Bowling Green pub.

**The Anchor Hotel reported as a hot bed of radicals and revolutionaries,
during the late 18th and early 19th centauries.**

Wharf Street had a notorious reputation, police never went there alone, a multitude of pubs existed in the warren of streets off it, One of them the Stag & Hounds, Providence Place, known locally as the Hen & Chicks had over the years gained a 'reputation'. When built it had its own stabling and brew house. During the 1840's the landlord was often fined for opening during prohibited hours, once a man had his bottom lip bitten off during a fight there.

The off-licence opposite the Stag and Hounds.

It was here in 1948 where what became known as 'The Battle of Providence Place' occurred. Bottles and razors were used when fighting in the Stag & Hounds spilled out into the street in front of the off licence opposite. The Leicester 'Flying Squad' police were called for to quell the violence. Six men were taken to hospital, one with his thumb almost severed. A total of nine people were charged and brought to court, which saw scenes almost as turbulent as the street fight. One woman fainted, another was removed from the court for shouting, and two men fined for assault were led away to the cells shouting that they would not pay.

The battle had been precipitated by a disturbance the previous weekend at the nearby Talbot pub, when windows had been broken. The Stag & Hounds was eventually closed in 1954. The whole of the area was to be cleared in the 'slum' clearance of the 1950's & 60's and with it went over 30 pubs to make way for the St Matthews Estate.

We've some fighting to do.

About ten years ago an elderly man recounted a story about his experience one evening in the Britannia Street, and Woodboy Street area, leading off Wharf Street, which had happened well over forty years before. He had recently been married and decided one night to go for a drink after work before heading home for his evening meal. He duly went into one of the many public houses in the area and started to drink his pint of beer. After a while a very large man entered the pub, he looked rather scruffy and was also covered in a large amount of blood. He tried to avoid any eye contact with the man, but the big man came over to him and insisted on buying him a drink He explained that he really had to go soon as his wife was cooking his dinner, but the man took no notice and he thought it was best not to start an argument with such an aggressive and large chap. He slowly drank the new pint of beer but was getting increasingly worried about this encounter, when he had nearly finished his drink he turned to the man, thanked him again and said that he must be getting back home. "Oh no you're not" he bellowed in reply, "You're coming with me". He again said that he was sorry but that he really did have to get home. "No you're coming with me, we've got some unfinished business to take care of, we have some more fighting to do"! It dawned on him that he had been recruited by this guy to help him continue a previous scrap. He managed to get to the outside toilet and was by this time in a state of total panic, there was only one front exit to the pub but it had a small court yard at the back surrounded by a high brick wall, he decided the only way of escape was over the wall. He flung his coat over the top of the wall (which had bits of old glass bottles embedded in it) and with adrenalin surging through his bloodstream some how managed to scramble up and over it. He ran as fast as could down a dark alleyway, into the street and all the way home. He dare not go out at night for weeks after that as he was so scared by the incident. From that day on he always carefully arranged his routes so that he would never again have to even walk past that particular pub.

Framework Knitting, The Luddites and the odd riot

The Globe 47, Silver Street.

The Globe circa 1900, apparently it was acquired by Everards in March 1906 for £7950.

The past history of the Globe reflects many aspects of the social background and development of Leicester. A large part of the working community were making a living from knitting using the wrought iron stocking frame invented by Lee in 1589. William Iliffe first introduced the frame to the county in Hinckley in 1640. It became a popular occupation for over two hundred years until mechanisation and the factories became established. The framework knitter's life was hard, working at home for extremely long hours, often with the assistance of all the family members. A practice termed scotch misting or soaping became widespread, this was achieved either by damping the materials or by using soap to add weight. This meant that some could be held back and the fraudulent material was sold at a cheaper rate. The distributors who encouraged this and sold on the finished "Black Market" items were called "turkey merchants"

About 1835 there is an account of an Abraham Stanley, landlord of a public house on the corner of Silver Street who was a distributor and was also a known "turkey merchant" .He had family connections with the trade, his sister was married to James Billings a trimmer and dyer of Rolls Court, Stockwell Head Hinckley. Abraham was later to become a hosier listed in 1846 as trading from South Bond Street. For many years the Globe was an important place for payment of wages and issue of work, with many of the men spending a good proportion of their income on beer. The payment of wages to workmen in public houses was a common practice until a bill was passed in 1882 to prohibit it. Nathaniel Corah started trading from the Globe in 1815, it was even by that time well established, as the meeting place for stockingers to gather to sell their goods. He would purchase the items and then transport them to Birmingham for finishing and dyeing as required. The business founded by him at one time employed over 2,000 people in Leicester at its peak.

A gravestone, which was set in the fireplace in the tap room, was removed in 1938 by workmen, the gravestone bore the names of Thomas and Katherine Cooke aged 11 and 4 respectively. Katherine died on March the first 1693. A listed building the Globe is a typical Georgian brick construction and plain design. At least two windows were bricked up following the introduction of the window tax in 1770. In the cellar there was well 160 feet deep to clear spring water, this was used at a time when the pub brewed its own beer and is very likely from the same source as the "Cank well."

The interior of The Globe looking much like someone's living room, surprisingly taken in the 1960's.

A contented customer having a little nap in the Globe taken in 2003, with his apt reading material, *'The very best of, last of the summer wine'.*

The Background

The history of the framework industry is long and complicated. It brought about both good and bad times for those employed in it. Prior to mechanisation all the members of the family carried on the work at home. It was subject at times to over production and greed from the Hosiers who rented out the knitting frames at a fixed weekly rate, regardless of the amount of work available and supplied the materials. Often having paid their costs the workers were left with a pittance to live on. Indeed it was in the frame owners interest to encourage even more workers as the frame rent revenue returned a most handsome return on their investment. Many of the workers themselves added to the problem as most were illiterate and poor with large families to keep. The children were working from an extremely early age and grew up to carry on the only trade they knew- they became more framework knitters. About the turn of the 19th century things got progressively worse with an increased labour force returning from the Napoleonic wars and simple changes in fashion. Trousers became the norm and the practice for gents to wear long socks all but vanished. The report of the commission into the plight of the Midland Framework Knitters showed that between 1815 and 1819 the average wage for working 15 hours a day had fallen by half! Those who ended up in the then local Parish Workhouses were put to work making more unwanted products. These could be sold at an even lower price, (no wages were paid to the inmates) which just made matters worse.

Framework Knitting in a Cottage in Enderby- an engraving by C.M. Pott

Many reports exist from that period, perhaps the most incisive one was written by William Felkin who visited a Leicester knitter in 1844: '*A female was at work between nine and ten at night: her husband and two journeymen at work above her head up the stepladder over the kitchen she was occupying. Her age she stated to be fifty-three: she had the appearance of being seventy: there were bones, sinews, and skin, but no appearance of flesh. She had been the mother of fifteen children, ten of whom, male and female, her husband and herself had bred up to be stockingers. From sickness in the morning, she could not work before her breakfast of tea, but laboured at night till ten o'clock. She had worked the same machine for 19 years and her clear earnings per week were 2s,6d.*' Children started to work from the age of 5 or 6 at winding and seaming.

Ok let's have a riot or two

In 1773 two local hosiers tried to introduce a new and improved stocking frame, totally ill conceived rumours spread that it could do the work of sixty men. About a thousand men descended into the Market Place where the mew machine was being displayed at the Old Exchange building . Someone through up a football and this was taken as a signal for the riot to kick off. The Mayor appeared and tried to reason with them and suggested they came inside to view it. Instead the ringleaders stormed the building and dragged out the machine, which was promptly smashed to pieces by the crowd.

In 1787 Joseph Brookhouse a local inventor went into partnership with two friends from the Unitarian Great Meeting John Coltman and Joseph Whetstone designing a new spinning machine. On hearing about a possible threat to their livelihood the local workers headed to Mr Whetstones house and then on to Coltmans where they smashed his windows and gutters. Mr Whetstone fearing there return removed the ladies from the house and with family and friends took up position upstairs armed with fowling pistols.

The house was of an old design with the top floor overhanging the lower. When the mob returned, by this time many of them were drunk, they managed to shelter under the overhang and broke into the ground floor and smashed up all the furniture. Mr Whetstone escaped down a rope from a rear window of the building and rode off on a borrowed horse.

At least one of them was taken to the infirmary with gun shot wounds. The Mayor eventually arrived with a few constables and tried to calm things down but with no avail. He then started to read the Riot Act but was hit on the head by a stone. It must have been a little bigger than a pebble because he subsequently died from the injury. After a long delay the militia were brought in, but the rioting lasted for another ten days. As a direct result of these troubles, worsted spinning was driven out of Leicester for more than twenty years.

A STATEMENT of the number of Stocking-makers now receiving regular weekly relief from the parish of St. Margaret's Leicester, whose average earnings do not exceed more than six shillings and sixpence per week when fully employed; with the number of children they have to support by their hand labour; and the assistance from the parish taken.

March 20th, 1819.

Men and Women with full Employ.				Total Number in Family.					
Nº 1. Benjamin Underwood	-	-	Wife and	4 Children	-	-	-	-	6
2. William Cockayne	-	-	Dº	5	Dº	-	-	-	7
3. James Wilbour	-	-	Dº	-	-	-	-	-	2
4. Thomas Gaskin	-	-	Dº	4	Dº	-	-	-	6
5. Thomas Lount	-	-	Dº	2	Dº	-	-	-	4
6. Thomas Clay	-	-	Dº	4	Dº	-	-	-	6
7. Edward Wooley	-	-	Dº	3	Dº	-	-	-	5
8. James Oldershaw	-	-	Dº	6	Dº	-	-	-	8
9. Martha Langton	-	-	Dº	2	Dº	-	-	-	3
10. Wᵈ Goodman	-	-	Dº	1	Child	-	-	-	2
11. Samuel Stretton	-	-	Dº	3	Children	-	-	-	5
12. Benjamin Ayres	-	-	-	-	-	-	-	-	1
13. Henry Waterfield	-	-	Dº	3	Dº	-	-	-	5
14. Thomas Allen	-	-	Dº	5	Dº	-	-	-	7
15. Samuel Loasby	-	-	Dº	1	Child	-	-	-	3
16. William Reynolds	-	-	Dº	4	Children	-	-	-	6
17. George Fenton	-	-	Dº	-	-	-	-	-	2
18. John Goodman	-	-	Dº	4	Dº	-	-	-	6
19. Henry Taylor	-	-	Dº	5	Dº	-	-	-	7
20. James Johnson	-	-	Dº	1	Child	-	-	-	3
21. John Baum	-	-	Dº	6	Children	-	-	-	8

Some of the framework knitter's names forwarded to the select committee looking into their grievances. (*Appearing at number 5 is a member of the Barry Lount clan*).

Lion & Lamb Horsefair Street, Gallowtree Gate corner.

The Lion & Lamb, this picture is of the one built in the 1740's on the site of the original. It was a major Inn during late Georgian times with its own stables and blacksmiths. It later became a stronghold of the Revolution Club.

A Celebration or Riot?

Christmas 1966 around the Clock Tower, pubs were packed with revellers breaking up from work on Friday 23rd. Trouble started in the White Horse near the Tower on Belgrave Gate, customers dived for cover as fighting erupted, tables were overturned and thrown around, it was estimated over 200 glasses were broken. The Fighting spilled out on to the street, where gangs of youths clashed around the Clock Tower.

Someone fell or was pushed through the nearby shoe shop window, gangs roamed the centre, one group broke into a store and stole liquor. Police were called to over 100 incidents, they described the events as "a disgrace to the city" The Leicester Mercury quoted a pub customer describing what took place as "a Roman orgy". All this took place unbelievably one lunchtime, (well England had won the world cup that year.)

The Yanks are coming!

1944 saw an influx of American service men to Leicester, many stationed on the outskirts in Knighton, Oadby and Stoughton They were well received on the whole, the 'yanks' generosity endeared them to the locals especially the girls and youngsters, who's query 'got any gum chum' was mostly met with some gift of sweets. There was a downside, mainly for the teenage local lads in the town, where the saying 'over paid, over sexed and over here' was apt, regular skirmishes in and around the town centre pubs took place. The townies could not compete financially with the yanks, they took exception to the local girls mixing with the GI's so flexing their prowess in fights was a way of proving the Leicester boys manliness. The girls didn't need protecting however, against a backdrop of war and rationing the yanks offered excitement and more, many local girls married and started a new life in the States.

Official fights were arranged at Joe Jacobs, Haunch of Venison on High Street. between the boxing locals and the yanks. Unofficial fights were everywhere else especially in Humberstone Gate around the Palais de dance, where the jitter-bug the new dance bought over by the yanks was the craze. Generally the GI's were well received, a few good books have been written on their stay in Leicester notably Baggy Pants & Warm Beer by Peter Outridge and Put on your Boots and Parachutes by Derrick Wills.

A darker side to some of the American psyche was the racism between themselves, which shocked the locals. On one occasion a group of American officers were drinking in a pub when a convoy stopped outside, two black drivers called in for some refreshment, the GI drivers ordered a drink from the landlord, when one of the officers shouted "no landlord we don't want any of those in here" the landlord replied "they only want a drink." "Serve them and we all leave" threatened the officer, the black drivers turned to leave saying "sorry boss we don't want any trouble", "wait" called the landlord "you gentlemen have asked for a drink and a drink you will have". At this point the party of American officers got up and left with the threat that the pub would be boycotted, leaving a few bemused locals who had never seen coloured guys before, and two black GI's standing at the bar. "Now gentlemen what can I get you."

Before the end of the war and the return home of the yanks stationed in Leicester, tensions between some locals who objected to their presence would erupt, sometimes between the GI's themselves, on a couple of occasions it unfortunately resulted in the death of an American soldier.

The Old Dixie Arms

The Old Dixie Arms Humberstone Road was one the pubs frequented by the GI's who would 'pawn' their watches for whisky to redeem when they got paid. One 'incident' tragically ended with the death of a black GI who was stabbed, the landlord was visited by the secret service police, who was told to hush up the death so as not to incite any racial violence in the American forces. The case was never fully reported.

Eventually the troops returned home but were replaced by a new influx of peacetime yanks stationed at Bruntingthorpe Aerodrome. With plenty of time and money on their hands, some pubs in the city centre once again became volatile. Leicester townies needed no excuse for a good punch up, Rock and Roll had arrived, and once again the Palais was thriving, pitch battles took place outside in Humberstone Gate.

The scene of many a punch up

One answer the Americans had was their own Military Police who would trawl the town centre in a jeep, two massive MPs one usually white the other black, who dolled out instant justice to any of their men who stepped out of line, (they never got involved with the locals). A lot of the GI's would congregate near the station in the Cosmo Club, usually 'the blood wagon' in attendance to quell any disturbance. Eventually the yanks returned home, leaving the locals to fight amongst themselves!

1964 was the year, The Admiral Nelson, Humberstone Gate, was the centre of the storm.

Recent immigration had begun to upset some locals who objected to 'certain' people using their pub. The landlord's solution was to make his lounge 'White Only' demonstrations, picketing and petitions against the Nelsons colour bar soon took place; students from Leicester University forced the issue when they crowded into the pub causing mayhem. After months of campaigning and protests the landlord finally caved in by lifting the ban. It ended one of Leicester's most unsavoury episodes, in all its pub history.

4
Sporting Tales

If bull and bear baiting are banned what will be next?

Will angling or foxhunting also be outlawed?

Attempts had been made in the early 1800's to ban many blood sports including those of baiting tethered animals by vicious, specially bred dogs. Unfortunately, the authorities failed to prevent it so the practice continued. There was much discussion both for and against banning such popular blood sports which had become established over hundreds of years.

Almost any animal was used from the 12th century until the early 19th century for brutal forms of 'entertainment' and, inevitably, for the associated betting and this included both bear and bull baiting. Bull baiting was more common practice, as bulls were readily to hand and cheaper to replace than bears. Badger baiting, cock fighting, dog fighting - even monkey and lion-baiting was not unusual – and members of the Royal Family attended these functions. There was an established position at Court known as Keeper of the Royal Bears.

The best fighting cocks were only bred by the very wealthy and were prized possessions. The obituary of the Earl of Derby, who died in 1834, stated his passion for horse racing but his more absorbing pastime was cock-fighting. He had a reputation for possessing the finest bred cockerels in England and even held cockfights in his own dining room, somewhat to his wife's annoyance. Although the well-to-do effectively organised and ran these events, they were for the most part open to people from every strata of society.

Purpose built bear gardens were constructed especially for such events; some very grand ones, tiered and circular in appearance (a miniature coliseum) holding around one thousand spectators. Indeed, most major towns owned something similar.

The original site of Leicester's bear garden is somewhat unclear. In 1260 the Borough Records mention "Berehill" situated close to the Haymarket, more or less where the Clock Tower stands today. This was later known as Bear Hill and Coal Hill in the 1700's. It has been argued that this was the site, however, Berehill has also been interpreted as derived from the Saxon term meaning 'agricultural produce' - barley in particular - making its position close to the old Haymarket a feasible alternative. Further from the town, Berehill Cross is mentioned in 1493 records. This large grass mound, surmounted by a cross, might well be the original site of a bear garden.

Bear baiting

It is probable that Leicestershire was the first County in England to actually exhibit bear baiting. King John was said to have been delighted to attend a bear-bait in Leicestershire. It was probable that bull baiting was also carried out at the same venue as both required the same basic seating facilities and a hefty stake with which to attach the unfortunate animal. Records of the Corporation Accounts for the year 1611 give details of rents received for the bear garden. Incredibly, bears were even baited during the Mayor's banquet as an amusing distraction between courses!

Hogarth's depiction of a London cock-pit

Leicester's cock pit with its' domed roof was situated on, or close by, the site now occupied by the Turkey Café in Granby Street. A later cock-pit was established at the Saracens Head (now Molly O'Grady's) on Hotel Street. Cock fighting and other blood sports were prohibited by Oliver Cromwell for a short period in 1654 but never really lost its' popularity and, in 1774, an advert appeared in the Leicester Journal inviting citizens to one such event on the 16th and 17th of February:

"Annual cocking will be fought at the Saracens Head Leicester. A main of Cocks between the gentlemen of the town and the gentlemen of the county, Mee and Glover feeders. N.B. There is now selling wholesale at the Saracens Head Inn a quantity of old Jamaica rum, and some exceedingly good brandies".

In the 1770s, a cockpit was sited where the City Rooms currently stands on Hotel Street. William Gardiner* stated that on occasions no fewer than one hundred cockerels would be slaughtered in the course of one day.

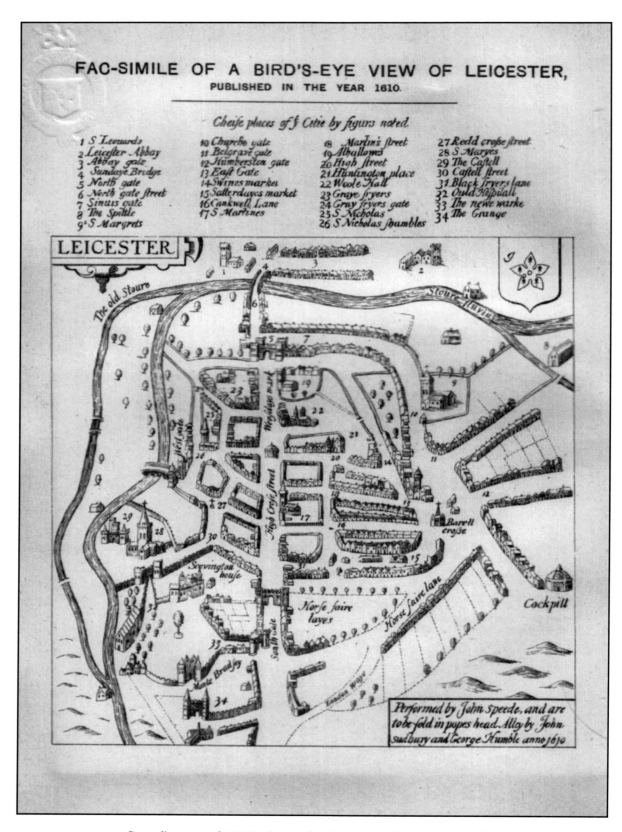

FAC-SIMILE OF A BIRD'S-EYE VIEW OF LEICESTER,
PUBLISHED IN THE YEAR 1610.

Speed's map of 1610. the cock-pit is just below centre right.

The old Saracen's Head on Hotel Street.

Next door is R.L. Atkinson's provisions shop, "Stilton House". Obviously, it sold cheeses but also a variety of other produce including ham, salmon, lobster and pickles.

There is no doubt that cock-fighting is a barbarous sport. However, it had strict and complex rules that demonstrated advanced thinking compared to human prize fighting bouts of the period. Cockerels were methodically matched in size and weight and a "count to ten" was introduced in order to give birds a chance to 'recover' or, more probably, die! It was some time before boxing caught up and adopted some of cock fighting's rules and to this day we refer to the weight classes as being either featherweight or bantamweight; terms which betray their origins.

The cock-fighting season generally began on Shrove Tuesday, with fights staged between various horse races at tracks across the country.

As part of the farming tithes, or rents, many landlords required farmers provide bulls for baiting. A gruesome proclamation, issued in Leicester during the year 1467 stated: *"The Mayor commandeth on the King's behalf that no butcher kill no bull within this town without it being baited before"*.

It was considered the flesh of a baited bull would be more tender and (in some subtle way) the mayor's proclamation ensured a plentiful supply of bulls being provided without incurring undue strain on the town's coffers!

At the Battle of Agincourt (1627) Leicester militia men bore their standards to battle. The banners depicted a fighting bull mastiff. Such was the townsmen's pride in blood sport.

In is recorded that in the year 1828 a particularly cruel act was carried out at a public bull baiting. The bull's tongue was cut out and paraded around on a platter in the hope of acquiring tips from the spectators. This, and other acts perpetrated against innocent animals was the subject of debate in Parliament and reinforced the determination of members to pass an act the banning of these dreadful "sports". It would seem that the public conscience was turning against such things and further legislation was passed in the Act of 1848, effectively put an end to cock fighting and all other forms of animal baiting.

The Saracen's Head circa 1992. Re-built in 1904 by architects Stockdale Harrison & Co. Erected, largely, on the site of the older building in the arts and crafts style. It was renamed as Molly O' Grady's in the late 1990's.

Did you know?
On the 14th of February 1798 the Corporation ordered that the Swine's Market be removed to the yard at the Saracen's Head, at the request of the occupier of that Inn, Mr Neal - and that this be advertised in the Leicester Journal.

In the Leicester Journal of 16th August 1787 there is an article referring to: "a fine young bear called Harry" who was kept in a Leicester Inn. Harry acted in the capacity of waiter and carried out his duties with "wonderful docility" The publisher of the Journal claims to have dined there whilst Harry was waiting tables. Being a favourite with the customers Harry was, unfortunately, often plied with ale. Over time, Harry became addicted and his behaviour grew ever more boisterous so that, eventually, the landlord was obliged to part with him! A subsequent report by Robert Read, sometime in the late 1780s reads:

"A frolicsome bear has lately been playing 'Old Harry' around the Full Moon in Russell Square; even a mild performing bear is now a great curiosity".

The Full Moon Russell Square, later demolished.

Did you know?

In 1791 Stafford Magistrates issued an order "to be stuck up in all public houses". All alehouses must close by ten o'clock in the evening from September to April or eleven from April to September. No Liquor could be drawn or sold during Devine Service on the Lord's Day. Every species of unlawful games be avoided; such as billiards, cards, cock fighting, skittles &c.

'They've banned our baits and cockfights, so a-ratting we shall go!'

Not to be utterly deprived of bloody pastimes, the gentle townsfolk of Leicester - being a resourceful bunch - turned their attention to ratting.

A rat pit was constructed in Soar Lane into which dogs would be thrown, together with a quantity of live rats and timed to see how many they could dispatch within a set period. An alternative was to put both dog and rats into a closed sack, to achieve the same result.

The Soar Lane rat pit, ratting continued there until after the end of the First World War. It was said to have been; *"patronised by dog fanciers from the nobleman down to the nailer."*

A Leicester 'sporting legend' was born on the 6th of August 1890. Called Jerry, he was a terrier owned by one Tom Withers, landlord of the Griffin Inn from 1895 to 1904. Jerry became the 'Champion Ratter of England' and was often seen performing his skills at the rat-pit in Soar Lane. A splendid poster of him exists at the Ship Inn on Soar Lane.

It was claimed that Jerry could kill five rats in ten seconds and once managed to kill fifty in a little over four minutes. So fearless and quick was he that, eventually, he became banned from contests and was forced to cross the Atlantic in order to continue his career in America. However, he proved too good for his own good there as well and was banned from performing. Jerry ultimately returned to Leicester and after his death was stuffed, mounted and displayed in a glass case for posterity at a public house off the Humberstone Road.

Circa 1900. The roughly cobbled Bedford Street, showing the entrance to The Griffin Inn on Belgrave Gate which was Jerry's home.

Did you know?

A Mr Warren recalled that once a month at the Old Talbot public house on Duns Lane a smartly dressed rat – catcher would arrive on Sunday lunchtime. He had a sack on his back, and when he entered the bar the customers would all stand on their seats. "The man would take his coat off and put his false teeth on the bar, put his hand in the sack and bring out three big rats which he let free in the bar. He would afterwards stalk them on his hands and knees and worry them with his gums". This was all done for charity and he would collect donations from the bar and smoke room.

A 'champion ratter' with his slaughtered rodents!

Did you know?

When the engineer, writer and historian R.T.C. Rolt passed through Leicester in 1939 on his narrow boat he was not at all impressed. He describes the County Arms at Blaby as a monster `gin palace` which looked like a factory, "The friendly, intimate atmosphere of the English Inn was entirely lacking, and the quality of the beer was execrable". On leaving the city things went from bad to worse! "We found that Belgrave Lock, through which we had to pass to rejoin the river was full of dead rats. The churning of our screw had sent their bloated, putrefied bodies bobbing up and down in horrid semblance of human life. Had there been a local rat week? we wondered". Two fishermen who sat on the bank seemed oblivious to all this and Rolt went on to say "They appeared to accept the malodorous corpses as part of the normal course of things. Perhaps Leicester breeds a fortuitous indifference to the more unpleasant aspects of city life".

Punch ups and Pork Pies

The Queens Head, mentioned in records of 1688, of which John Vain was landlord in the early 1700s, was later named The Castle Tavern and situated at number 43 Gallowtree Gate. By the middle of the 19th century The Castle was being run by Richard (Dick) Cain, an Irishman born in Dublin around the year 1819.

Nat Langham

As well as running The Castle Tavern, Dick was a pugilist and set up his sparring and training rooms at the tavern and it was here that Dick became the mentor and promoter of Nathaniel (Nat) Langham.

Nathaniel Langham was born at Hinckley on 20th May 1820. His parents were described as 'drunken paupers' and Nat was so neglected as a child that he was reduced to eating scraps of food left for the dog. As a boy, he was once caught stealing a hot potato from a market cart. By way of punishing him, the incensed potato-vendor thrust the hot potato into Nat's mouth, so severely burning him that for ever after he suffered a speech impediment.

Nat was a middle-weight (bare knuckle) prize fighter and the only person to beat Tom Sayers (who was the first man ever to be declared a boxing World Champion). Nat, himself, was the English champion, an obvious favourite and hero with the people of Leicester who turned out in great numbers to watch him fight.

In time, Nat moved to London presumeably for greater prize money. He challenged and fought Tom Sayers at Lakenheath on 18th November 1853. Incredibly, the fight lasted over two hours and it was not until the 61st round that Tom, finally, threw in the towel! He retired and that same year married Elizabeth Watson. He was to give his address as: St Martins Lane, probably the Coach and Horses, as he also gave his profession as 'Licensed Victualar'. The witness at his wedding was his trainer, Ben Caunt, who was also a champion pugilist.

The contest against Tom Sayers at Lakenheath was by no means the longest fight Nat undertook.

NAT LANGHAM V TOM SAYERS.

The following is an extract from an article published in The Times in 1914, comparing the pros and cons of more modern boxing contests with those of the pugilists:

recovery. The ancient battles often went on hour after hour until the two men were too tired to deliver an effective blow. Thus the fight between Nat Langham and Harry Orme in 1851 lasted three hours and 117 rounds. Towards the close the men could hardly stand. and practically had to be carried up to the scratch by their seconds. They could no longer hit ; they could only shove one another about feebly. In the last round Langham tried to push Orme over, not seeing that he was out of reach. He fell, and, being unable to rise again, was a loser for the first and last time in his much-enduring life.

Did you know?

In 1932 an elderly man called Talbot who was in his 88th year and lived in Brandon Somerset recalled an itinerant tinker who lead his wife with a halter up Market Street. He then sold her for half a crown. The purchaser who was another travelling salesman then took her away in his cart. He also remembers as a boy seeing Tom Sayers being led away with a rug over his head after being defeated by the fists of Nat Langham.

From about 1856, Nat became the Landlord of a London public house called the Cambrian Stores at 13, Castle Street, St Martin's in the Fields, Westminster. However, in 1860 his request to renew his pub's license was turned down – as was his appeal against this ruling several weeks later – and it may have been his disappointment which drove him to come out of boxing retirement and return to Leicester, where he teamed up once again with Dick Cain at the Castle Tavern.

(The following letter to the The Times newspaper in 1860 gives a graphic insight into electrifying atmosphere to be found at Nat Langham's pub):

The Cambrian Stores was what is called "a fighting-house". It was frequented by pugilists, and by their associates. It was kept open all night. The preliminaries of prize-fights were arranged there, the combatants made their deposits there, they weighed there the day before they fought, they showed there the day after the battle, they took their benefits there. There was sparring, singing and dancing there every night. The dancing – chiefly "clog-hornpipes" on tables – was of the heaviest and noisiest description, especially when it was indulged in by a powerful negro performer known as "Langham's fancy black". On "weighing days" on "fighting days" and on "settling days" before, during and after every great fight, between 2,000 and 3,000 of the lowest and most lawless ruffians London could produce, swearing, struggling, sparring and shouting, crowded the "stores" and streets around in such masses as to set the police at defiance, and to compel the terrified neighbours to close their shops. Over this pandemonium Nat Langham an ex-pugilist and licensed victualler, presided".........

Small wonder then that the authorities wanted the Cambrian Stores shut down!

The fight between Nat Langham and Tom Paddock, promoted by Dick Cain, took place at the Leicester Cricket Ground. The year was 1860 and it was the last that Nat Langham was ever to fight.

Whatever the conclusion of the license argument, Nat continued to live at the Castle Street address and is described in the 1861 census as a 'widower, aged 40, victualler at the Cambrian Stores.' Residing with him were his daughter, aged six; his brother Samuel; two seventeen-year old barmaids, and a waiter. He was still at that address when the 1871 census was taken. However, he died of consumption later that same year and was buried at Brompton Cemetery.

Jem Mace, who was the champion of England in 1861 and '62, apparently served his apprenticeship in the boxing booth of Nat Langham.

Nat's opponent, Tom Paddock

Tom Paddock was nicknamed the 'Redditch Needlemaker', he had an uncontrollable temper and had once served ten months' hard labour for instigating a riot at one of his contests.

Did you know?

The Queensbury rules for the sport of boxing were published in 1867. Rule number five is as follows; a man hanging on the ropes in a helpless state, with his toes off the ground, shall be considered down.

(seems a bit harsh!)

The pork pie poisoner

Changes were afoot for The Castle public house in Gallowtree Gate, Leicester when, in May 1873, the landlord from the World's End pub took over its' license.

Two years later, John Crowhurst who managed the Robin Hood pub, applied for a 'change of use' in order to open a restaurant on the adjacent site. This was agreed and the name was changed to The Criterion.

The Criterion was described as an opulent establishment, with marble topped counters and tables. It still retained a liquor license and in 1881 featured in the great scandal of the "Pork Pie Poisoner". An 'outraged' press reported the incident

"The whole town was in a fever of excitement over the seizure of 2-3 tons of putrified pork, bacon and other meat on the premises of Viccars Collyer of Silver Street next door to the Opera House."

Viccars Collyer was a wholesale provisions merchant, bacon and cheese factor trading from 24 Silver Street and from the premises next door at number 22, known as Central Hall. He lived at Highfield House, 2 Titchbourne Street and he is recorded to be residing at that address in the 1881census. He was a provisions merchant and confectioner employing thirty-four men and seven boys. In the same year, he advertised his small selection box as one of his 'sensible Christmas presents'. It cost 5s 6d., and consisted of a 3lb pork pie, 1lb sausages, 1lb iced cake, a dozen mince pies and a large Leicester cake. It also included a free box and a delivery service anywhere in Leicester.

The condemned rotten meat had, apparently, been intended for his sausages and the manufacture of his Christmas pork pies! Through the diligence of a local health inspector a maggoty mess was discovered, described as being in a 'high state of putrification' and was removed to the Town Hall in carts, where it lay awaiting official inspection and exposed to the elements, giving off such obnoxious odours that it turned the stomachs of all in the vicinity.

The word - and the smell (!) quickly spread and Collyer, who was on his way to the police station, was recognised by the crowd who hounded and chased him with cries of: 'lynch him' and 'lets rip him up'. Viccars, wisely, decided to take refuge in The Criterion.

He appeared in court on 9th January 1880 facing charges on twenty-five counts regarding the sale of eight and a half hundredweight of diseased and rotten meat. He and his partner, Dunmore, were fined £200.

Severe damage had been done to the pork pie industry and repeated attempts were made to reassure the public. One advert at the time stated:

The Belvoir pork pie.

The makers of the above will give £100 if any person can prove that they are using or have ever have had used other than fresh English Pork.

Viccars appears to have ceased trading as a pork pie maker not long after the court case (can't imagine why). However he continued trading as a florists and nurseryman with premises listed at Glenfield and at 22 Silver Street in 1885. In 1891 he was living with his wife and family in Glenfield with his sons trading as seedsmen, nurserymen and agriculteral equipement dealers.

The Criterion failed to renew its' public house license in 1899 but continued for a few years afterwards as a restaurant.

The Criterion (circa 1900)

Several other Leicester pubs were known for their boxing connections, most notably The Bath Hotel in Bath Lane, The Jolly Angler in Wharf Street, The Haunch of Venison in High Street and The Antelope in Silver Street. Latterly, the old Robin Hood in Woodgate, The Hunters Rest (formerly The Blue Moon) in Carlisle Street and The Uppingham in Uppingham Road have all housed training gyms for boxers.

Joe Jacobs ran The Haunch of Venison for almost 20 years and was a major player in boxing circles. At least one boxing club remains – The Fountain Boxing Club to the rear of The Fountain pub on Humberstone Gate.

The Bath Hotel was not as salubrious as it might sound. It was situated on Bath Lane near the West Bridge and was run for many years by Bill Sherriff, a former champion boxer who, in Victorian times, fought under the name of 'Young Bruce'.

**One of Bill Sherriff's
Boxing trophies**

**The Bath Hotel
(originally The Boat & Engine)**

Barry Lount's father Cyril was, for a time, brought up at the Bath Hotel by his Uncle Bill Sherriff and his Aunt Ada (nee Lount) who ran The Bath from 1907 until 1926. They regaled Cyril with their stories whilst plying him with a 'giant lumps' of Ada's cake. He also remembers, as a young boy, watching men knock 'ten bells' out of one another in the pub's boxing booth and meeting many of the characters who frequented The Bath Hotel. Bill Sherriff was often in trouble with the law, usually for poaching offences. No-one dared enter Bill's living quarters un-invited for not only did they have Bill to contend but also his two Lurcher hounds which were always ready for the kill! On one occasion in 1915 Bill was threatened with twenty-eight days in prison for allowing drinking on the pub's premises during prohibited hours.

As is the case with so many 'hard' men Bill had his soft side. He and Ada took great pleasure from Bill's large aviary where a variety of song birds, including Linnets, were kept. As a boy, Barry would gaze in admiration at this large gentle man who, with hands like dustbin lids, would softly handle and talk to his birds.

Bill Sherriff, a former Champion Boxer, in his later years

The Jolly Angler public house on Wharf Street housed an upstairs boxing gym.

The Jolly Angler - a very 'basic boozer' - although this photograph taken sometime in the 1960s gives a somewhat different impression. The white facade was added during the early 30s. In early Victorian times, The Jolly Angler brewed its own beer. However, it ceased brewing in 1888 when the plant and equipement were auctioned off.

Another pub known for its boxing gym was the Antelope in Silver Street.

Above: the interior circa 1964

**Left: The Antelope, awaiting its' fate
in the early 1970s.**

First records of The Antelope public house go back as far as 1666. It possessed its' own brew-house and, most notably, completely lacked a bar as all the beer pumps were mounted on the wall. It had its' own stabling and coaches ran regularly to and fro from to Coventry and Birmingham.

Around 1958 a boxing gym opened under the auspices of the landlord Fred Mobbs and many famous boxers trained there, including Wally Swift, Johnny Prescott, Jack Bodell and Richard Dunn, all of whom were top fighters in their day.

The years after the Great War saw many working men's clubs staging boxing competions and Leicester's premier club at this time was Spinney Hill Working Mens' Club. Other popular venues for boxing in Leicester in the 1920s and '30s were the Belgrave, the City of Leicester and the Gypsy Lane Working Mens Clubs. Matches were also held at the Cossington Street Baths and the Free Trade Hall.

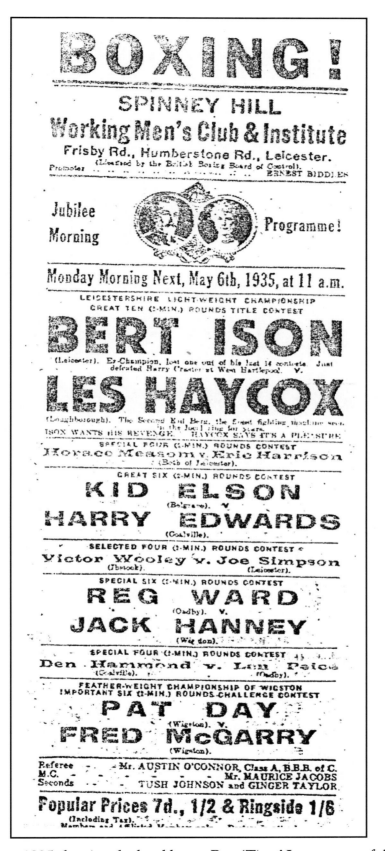

Poster from 1935 showing the local boxer, Bert 'Tiger' Ison, as top of the card.

Bert 'Tiger' Ison recorded three hundred and thirty seven fights during his career; many at Working Mens' Clubs. Yet, even Bert did not match up to the incredible Len Wickwar on his total number of fights.

Those Leicester boxers who each recorded over one hundred fights during their careers included Pop Newman - the Newman family own and manage the very popular Newman's Café, in Market Street, where photos of Pop are to be seen adorning the walls. Pat Butler, Horace Barber, Bill Hardy, Harry Lem, Colin McDonald and Ric Sanders must also be included in Leicester's rich source of boxing talent.

The Friar Tuck public house ran a boxing gym during the 1920s and this was where the incomparable Len Wickwar trained. Len had the distinction of producing the most recorded fights in boxing history. He amassed an incredible total of four hundred and sixty seven fights during the 1920s and '30s.

The Friar Tuck had another unique claim to fame; an iron stove – which had no chimney – was to be found on the bar! Sadly, the establishment's reputation hit the rocks in March 2002 when two men were shot and another two stabbed in an after hours drinking brawl which saw the pub lose its license.

Another boxing connection was that of Alex Barrow, a Nigerian, who boxed out of Leicester in the late 1950s and 60s. Alex fought some of the country's top heavyweights of the day, such as Johnny Prescott and Joe Erskine. He later opened his own club, The Blue Beat. It was likely this establishment was, originally, the Stag public house, situated on Upper Conduit Street. (Barry Lount remembers having gone there on occasions).

Alex then opened a new club on the corner of Campbell Street, which he called: The House of Happiness – which might have been something of a misnomer!

The incomparable Len Wickwar

George Biddles business card which he used while he was based at the Dixie Arms in St Peter's Lane. George promoted many of Leicester's boxers throughout the years and produced several champions.

The Dixie Arms, St Peter's Lane.

Other boxing promoters and managers of recent memory who contributed greatly to the Leicester sporting scene were Johnny Griffin and Carl Gunns. Carl Gunns still runs a boxing gym in the area.

Post war champions featured among them Chris Pyatt, Tony 'Sibbo' Sibson, Rendall Munroe, Mick Greaves, Mick Basten, Tony McKenzie, Martin and Kevin Conception. Tim Wood, although he was London born, learned his skill in Leicester. Many of them graced the world stage and all could claim championships in their day. The list goes on; a complete book could be written on Leicester's boxers.

Eric Gibbins shows off 'Sibbo's belt

Mick Basten claims it suits him better

Football, wide-eyed and legless!

William "Billy" Banister joined Leicester Fosse Football Club, later the Leicester City Football Club, from Woolwich Arsenal in May 1904 for (at that time) a record club fee of £395. Banister was born in Burnley in 1879 and began his career there before moving to Bolton and Arsenal. He was a towering centre–half, who was capped twice for England and became the team's captain. He played his last game for Leicester against Wolves in June 1910 and, after a period in the reserves, was transferred back to Burnley. Towards the end of his career he played for Crewe before finally returning to Leicester and playing football for the Abbey Lane Imperials in 1913..

Billy ran pubs in Burnley and Leicester he was the landlord of the Woolcombers Arms on Church Gate. He died at the Woolcombers on 26th March 1942.

A rather forlorn looking Woolcombers Arms at 54, Lower Church Gate.

The photograph was taken circa 1969 shortly before the pub finally closed down. It had brewed its' own beer before 1906, when the All Saint's Brewery took over and later purchased the Lease.

Leicester Fosse playing at Filbert Street (circa 1890)

The away team's defence and goalkeeper appear more interested in the camera than in playing the game. Also, the goal-post upright seems to be supported by thick wire 'guide ropes', which could certainly cause injury – no Health & Safety legislation in those days!

One of Billy's team mates at Leicester Fosse was Robert Frewin Turner, known as 'Leggy' Turner, who was a swift outside-left player and a local lad. He first played for the club in September 1906. 'Leggy' then moved to Everton (in 1909) for a transfer fee of £700., a club record fee at the time and, shortly afterwards, scored one of the winning goals in a Leicester 3-2 triumph over Manchester United. Additionally, Turner proved a proficient cricket all-rounder, playing for his home County.

Team photograph for the 1905-6 Season

Middle row left, seated next to the trainer, is Bob 'Leggy' Turner and sitting in the centre of the picture is the Captain, Billy Banister, guarding the ball!

In 1909, an away match described by the Leicester Chronicle as "a farcically absurd game" took place against Nottingham Forest when Leicester Fosse lost 12-0 – an astounding club defeat. A hearing was called for by the Football League and held at the Grand Hotel where, it was discovered, the Leicester players had played the match in a state of collective inebriation. They had all been out on the town the evening prior to the match, celebrating their former team mate Leggy Turner's wedding. The Football League decided, wisely, to put their dozy performance down to hangovers! Unfortunately, further disappointment ensued when three days later a more sober Leicester team lost to Everton. Ironically, Everton's success was aided by their new signing – Bob 'Leggy' Turner.

Billy Banister, Captain of Leicester Fosse and one time Landlord of the Woolcombers Arms

Did you know?

In January 1903 Leicester had a good 3-1 away win over Burnley, but it could have been more. An excellent save was made when an on target shot hit a stray dog which was running across the oppositions goal mouth and deflected the ball clear.

Cricket, Lovely Cricket!

It is believed that cricket was first played in Leicestershire in the hunting districts, hence the adoption of the fox as the emblem for the club.

The balls were bowled under arm, the wicket had only two stumps, runs were recorded as notches and an over consisted of only four balls. However it provided a sport where large amounts of money could be won or lost. Betting prevailed and exposed the game to accusations of match fixing. So, in some respects nothing really changes.

Cricket was played on the St Margaret's Pastures in Leicester until a new ground was established on Wharf Street. The new venue became fashionable and was perceived as exclusive and the more wealthy players were quick to move there, leaving behind the local lads who still lacked the financial support and influence they themselves enjoyed. As a result, of course, the less well off players became marginalised and were restricted to using the older cricket grounds. (See "the conditions for the new Cricket Ground").

An early report in the Leicester Journal of 1780 reads; *'a match of cricket was played at St Margaret's Pasture betwixt 11 young men of Leicester and 11 of Loughborough which was won by the latter by more than fifty notches.'*

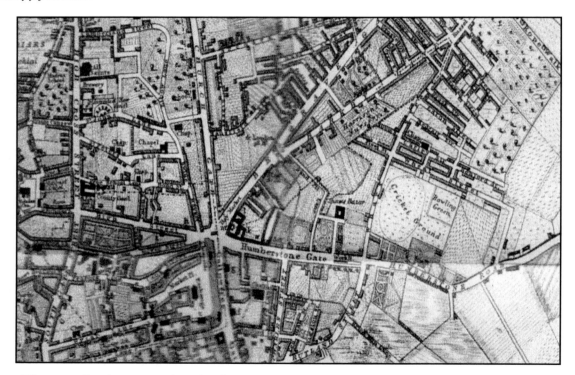

The new Cricket ground, Wharf Street, is clearly shown on Cockshaw's map of 1828.

In 1787, a grand cricket match was played in Hinckley on Monday 6th of August in a field adjoining the town. The Gentlemen of Leicester played the Gentlemen of Coventry for a total purse of 200 guineas. It was predicted prior to the game that this would be a great match and, given the agility of the players, would prove a "great sport was expected; and it is supposed a great concourse of people will attend the occasion". The odds were in favour of Leicester.

Leicester batted first and the eleven men managed to attain a grand total of 13 runs (or notches), which included one extra.

```
                                      LEICESTER
        Wm.  Barsby, b. Crump  ......      6
        Wm.  Clarke, b. Crump .........    o
        M.  Graham, b. Sparrow ......      1
        G.  Davis, b. Crump ...........    1
        John Shergold, run out .........   2
        C.  Wilkinson, b. Sparrow ......   1
        T.  Fielding, c. Crump .........   1
        E.  Higginson, b. Sparrow ......   o
        John Mitchell, c. Payton ......    o
        Wm.  Bates, not out ...........    o
        J.  Dufty, b. Crump ...........    o
                  Bye  Balls .............  1
                                          ——
                                          13
```

The dismal Leicestershire scorecard does not reflect the pre-match hype.

For some extraordinary reason this, bizarrely, proved to be part of a winning score! Perhaps the second innings was considerably better? As a consequence, when the Leicester players adjourned to a local pub a large-scale fight broke out with the Coventry supporters, many of whom were local colliers. A report in the local paper reads: *'a scene of bloodshed ensued, at present we haven't heard of any lives lost, though the weapons used were of the most dangerous and alarming'.*

The Leicester team managed to fight off their opponents and because many of them came from St Nicholas parish they gained the nickname of 'Nick's roughs'.

By 1825 the Corporation were in favour of building an enclosed cricket ground in the town. A proposal was put forward in May of that year by a consortium of four well-to-do businessmen to lease the ground for a period of ten years, with an option to re-let it after a short period on " terms they saw fit ". The offer was made on the condition that 'a commodious Inn or Hotel' would be purpose built alongside the ground. The building appears to have been seriously delayed, most probably through haphazard funding. It finally opened about 15 years later and was called the Cricketers' Hotel.

It was further suggested that: *"the Corporation should provide no other Cricket Ground to come into competition with this one".* As one of the consortium was Otway Cave who later and controversially was elected a Member of Parliament for Leicester the following year, they probably had their wish.

The Cricket Ground on Wharf Street finally opened in 1825 and managed from 1828-1839 by the publican of the Angel Inn on Gallowtree Gate, William Whitehead. William Barker, the licensee of the Anchor Inn on Charles Street, then took over the lease in 1840.

When cricket had been played on the St Margaret's Pastures, the aptly named Cricket Players public house on Church Gate was conveniently situated on the route to and from the town centre. It survives to this day.

During the 1840s, the Ancient Order of Druids would meet regularly at the Cricket Players pub.

The building has undergone many changes of name in recent history; The Long Stop; The Pinch of Snuff; Churchgate Tavern and (more recently) The Gatehouse.

The Cricket Players, Church Gate

William Barker, Licensee of the Anchor Inn was the entrepreneur of Leicestshire Cricket at the Wharf Street ground. Cannily, he held a second licence at the Cricketers' Hotel, which fronted onto Wharf Street from about 1842-1862. This attracted not only the players and supporters but also customers from the other events held on the ground. The Cricket Ground was run on a strictly commercial basis and various events were held there. Increasing, cricket became a game for the wealthy middle classes, with players paying a subscription and spectators being charged seven shillings for the Season.

Other entertainments held there included firework displays, bowls, pigeon shooting and pony racing in the winter. In October 1835 Mrs Graham attempted an ascent in a hot air balloon from the cricket ground. Unfortunately, the balloon's mooring rope was severed whilst crossing Wharf Street and the net encompassing the silk balloon became tangled round a chimney. The basket in which Mrs Graham was riding, hit a protruding drain-spout. The balloon shuddered and rolled violently and the chimney bricks proceeded to loosen. A large gash appeared in the silk. Finally, the residents of the house, through a back-bedroom window, rescued the terrified Mrs Graham.

In 1860 the lease of the Cricket Ground was taken on by Edward Morrell but later sold at auction to the Town Clerk for £5,600 who promptly re-sold it to developers. Such was the loss to the people of Leicester who had long enjoyed it as a place of entertainment. Over the next decade Leicester cricket declined, before re-emerging at Victoria Park in 1872.

There was one person who managed the transformation from humble beginnings, rising to exalted heights playing with his more wealthy teammates and that was Arthur Dick Pougher. Born in 1865, at 111 Humberstone Road, Pougher was later described as a Professional Cricketer. By that time he was about twenty-five years of age and living at 98, Livingstone Street with his wife Kate and daughter Rose. Their second child Arthur Dick named after his father was born about two years later in 1893.

The New Cattle Market Hotel (circa 1904) of which A.D. Pougher was the landlord until 1902. Originally a beer house it acquired a full licence in 1872. The building was demolished a century later for the purpose of road widening.

Described in 1927 as, arguably, the most famous of all Leicestershire cricketers, Pougher was the first Leicester player to score over 1,000 runs in first class cricket in a season. He took more than 1,200 wickets for 14 runs whilst playing for an England eleven against Surrey in 1895.

Appearing for the M.C.C. in 1896, he played in a team which included Dr W.G.Grace, gaining a sweet revenge against the visiting Australians who, in 1878, had dismissed the England team in one innings for a miserable 19 runs.

Pougher was brought on to bowl when the Australians had scored 18 in reply to England's first innings score of 219. He proceeded to bowl 3 overs, for no runs, and to take 5 wickets in a remarkable spell of bowling against the Australia opposition who were all out for 18.

It is worth noting that Leicestershire was the first England County cricket team ever to play against an Australian side (in 1878) when no fewer than twelve-thousand spectators turned up on the first day.

In 1894 Leicester were given First Class status and in their commencing match against Essex Pougher took 14 wickets and scored a century. He played a benefit match 1900, for which he received a cheque for £220 from the Leicester Club at the end of the Season. He continued playing cricket for Leicestershire until 1902.

Pougher was also the landlord of The Sir Robert Peel public house on Jarrom Street in 1892 and, during 1894, he took over the management of The New Cattle Market Hotel on the Aylestone Road. In the 1901 census he is still listed as being there - both as a professional cricket player and a licensed victualler - prior to moving in 1902 to The Old Cricket Ground Hotel on Grace Road, where he later died on 20th May. After Probate had been granted on 15th October 1926, his personal effects were valued at £1,688. 7s. 4d.

The Sir Robert Peel pub in Arthur Pougher's time

The 1888 Score Card; when Leicestershire beat the Australians in 1888, Pougher taking a total of 10 wickets in the match for 71 runs in 56 overs.

The many talents of Arnold Rylott

Arnold Rylott was born in 1839 and died in 1914, in his later life he was the licensee and brewer at The Earl of Leicester, Infirmary Square during the 1890s, until Everards bought the pub circa 1900. He then moved in with his brother Harris who was running the Royal Standard in Charles Street who had previously ran The George and Dragon, Peel Street for many years.

Arnold was a well known cricketer who played for Leicestershire from at least 1875 until the 1890s. As a fast left arm bowler he took 387 wickets for Leicester still holding the best ever average of all time of 14.77 runs per wicket taken. He was also an excellent right handed batsman scoring over 5,000 runs for the county. he played cricket for England in 1880.

Arnold was additionally an accomplished footballer playing half back for Grantham. He went on to become the head of ground staff at Leicester and also for a time at Lords cricket ground. He also found time to publish a book of verse and make a potent variety of snuff which he passed on to the other members of the Leicester cricket team. During the winter months he worked as a gamekeeper who allegedly wasn't adverse to a spot of poaching.

Billiards, Rugby and Beer

Billiards became extremely popular towards the end of the 19th century. Public houses then, as now, were eager to adapt to new innovations and the Barley Mow in Granby Street was one such Inn. Here, landlord Charles Wheatley advertised his fashionable 'Wheatley's Billiard Room'. Not to be out-done by this, The Granby coffee house further down the street also opened a 'Temperance Billiard lounge'. The Temperance Movement was gaining in strength at this time believing (and being proved right, at least in some instances) that the path of drink lead, ultimately, to damnation.

In 1880, The George Hotel in the Haymarket held an inaugural meeting of what was to become the Leicester Tigers. Indeed, The George ultimately became their headquarters.

The Welford Road Recreation Ground was the Tigers official home ground but having no club house or changing facilities, teams would have to change in the Bedford Hotel across the road, where rugby's association with drinking was already established. There were some complaints that no heating was provided on a bitterly cold days at the Bedford, despite the amount of business being generated by playing teams.

The Bedford, renamed the Victory after a Tigers Cup final win in the early 1980's.

Eddie Redman, a player in the 1890s was the landlord of the Welford Tavern whilst Captaining the Tigers.

Harry Wilkinson, another Tiger team member of the 1890s helped his parents run the Victoria Model Lodging House, in Britannia Street. (Both Harry and his brother Edwin played for the Tigers).

Irish immigrants, many of whom were escaping the potato famine of the mid-1800s occupied the majority of the lodging houses in the Belgrave Gate area. In some streets 25% of the population were Irish. The lodges were filthy, disreputable places where drunkenness, begging and prostitution were rife. A dozen people would be housed in one room. They were charged 2d. to lie down, or 1d. to sleep in a standing position draped over a rope!

The Wilkinson's lodging house was a better class of establishment. In 1881 it was recorded that there were fifty-five people lodging at the premises. None, however, were Irish immigrants. Generally, the Irish were discriminated against. An advertisement exists (from 1838) for a vacancy for a cook. Apart from being: *"A good cook who perfectly understands her business in all its branches"* she was: *"expected to make herself useful,"*. The mind boggles at what might be intended by the latter half of the statement. The advertisement concludes: *"No Irish need apply!"*

The Wilkinson's Model Lodging House, in Britannia Street. Rooms were let at a nightly rate. No smoking was not allowed, nor alcohol on the premises. The house was specifically designed to provide a better standard than those of the neighbouring lodges.

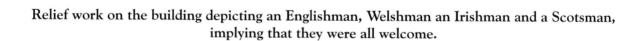

Relief work on the building depicting an Englishman, Welshman an Irishman and a Scotsman, implying that they were all welcome.

Conversely, Harry whilst still playing for the Tigers, and together with his brother Albert, took over as landlord and barman the Sultan Vaults, close to Belgrave Gate and a far cry from the Temperance regime prevalent at the Britannia Street Lodging House. The previous landlord of The Sultan had been fined for allowing drunkenness on the premises. Harry's last game for the tigers took place in 1905.

The Sultan boasted a range of bar games such as dominoes, cards, 'Devil Among the Tailors' and skittles. Apparently, the establishment smelled strongly of urine – not quite the required ambience for a romantic night out!

**The Sultan, much changed since Harry's time as the pub was rebuilt in 1931.
It ceased business in 1994.**

More Awful Sports

Another jolly pastime in 14th century Leicester, was the throwing of cudgels at live cockerels. These events took place in the Newarke. The unfortunate birds were tethered to prevent their escape whilst the participants hurled their clubs at them. The winner, of course, was the owner of the club that killed the bird, who would then be allowed to take his prize home and cook it. To the disappointment of many, this 'sport' was abolished in 1784.

However, there were other events, equally popular, taking place at the Newarke one of which was held at the time of the Shrove Tuesday Fair and was called: Whipping Toms. This was when the 'Toms' would attack the 'Players' with cart whips with the intention of playfully expelling them from the fairground. Any man remaining in the fairground after the two o'clock bell had sounded would be thoroughly "whipped". According to the somewhat whimsical rules of the game, the recipients should only be struck upon the legs – preferably below the knee – but such was the excitement of the moment that this rule was generally ignored and the entire game would descend into a mass brawl bordering on civil riot.

It is said that the vicar of St. Mary's church became involved in one such skirmish and was forced to run the gauntlet through the fairground to his vicarage gate. This annual form of letting off steam was prohibited in 1846 and the populous warned they would face fines of £5. apiece if there was any further breach of public order.

However, 'Nature Abhors a Vacuum' (as the saying goes) and when one form of recreation is abolished, another will almost certainly take its' place. Thus it was, that on Shrove Tuesday 1847, an enthusiastic group of men and boys gathered at the Newarke to kick a ball around. Some policemen, sensing impending trouble, attempted to put an end to what was, basically, an innocent activity; whereupon all hell let loose and it took the entire Borough Constabulary to quell the ensuing riot.

When Leicester folk were not hurling cudgels at benighted birds, or provoking the police, they were indulging in the game of 'Tailing the Cat'. A cat, or sometimes even a hare, would be drenched in aniseed, attached to a horse's tail and dragged through the streets, pursued by hounds. The ecstatic crowd following this fracas would then finish up at the Mayor's residence where a feast would have been laid on, and where ale would freely flow.

It would seem the town's population knew how to enjoy itself - although you would take a somewhat different view if you were a cat, or a chicken!

The Stag and Pheasant

A pub and hotel where many legends of the sporting world stayed, when they came to Leicester was the Stag & Pheasant in Humberstone Gate. Boxing Hero's Jack Dempsey, Len Harvey, Bombardier Billy Wells and Larry Gains all reputedly stayed at the Inn as well as top entertainers such as Gracie Fields.

Originally Georgian rebuilt in 1905 to become one of Leicester's leading taverns, it had its own grill room and champagne bar between the wars, it disappeared from Leicester's pub scene together with another dozen of the city's historic inns to make way for the 1960's new Haymarket 'development' (if you can call it that).

5
Fashionable 'Freaks'

Freak shows were a popular form of entertainment during the 18th century, indeed they didn't fully die out until the 1960's and even later in other parts of Europe. Leicester had its share, including the well-known pair of Daniel Lambert the 'fattest man in the world' and Joseph Merrick the 'Elephant man'. In addition to them others with physical deformities were often tied to travelling circuses. Some would also tour the country exhibiting themselves as individuals. The obvious place for this was the tavern or hotel, probably the origins of our modern day pay to view culture, which has become one popular source of our entertainment today.

Those who were described at the time as "Giants or Dwarfs" were always a popular attraction. One such gentleman was Patrick O'Brien the 'Irish Giant' The Leicester Journal advertised in October 1794 ' See the celebrated Irish giant, measures over 9 feet high. The most surprising man in the World. He will be seen at The Lion & Dolphin Leicester'.

The advert and posters embellished the truth somewhat, in fact when O'Brien died he was measured at 8ft 1 inch, still extremely tall, but never let the facts get in the way of a good tale and a making a few extra shillings. Patrick was buried in a lead coffin 12 feet down in rock to thwart the 'body snatchers'.

The "Yorkshire giant" William Bradley also travelled around the country at a similar period of time he was seven feet nine inches high and joined Barnum's circus. He was often exhibited with the enormous monster " The Great Yorkshire Pig". William was a committed teetotaller unlike Edwin Calvert who came from the next village to him he was only thirty six inches high and was also exhibited around the country until his death from excessive drinking at the age of 17! William Bradley died in 1820 aged 33, again worried in case of body snatchers his grave was guarded for several weeks, then the coffin was exhumed and re- buried inside the Church in his home town of Market Weighton under a marble slab. He was recorded as England's tallest man until at least 1996 and may still hold that record.

Leicester Market Place with the Lion & Dolphin on the right.

Charles Byrne (1761–1783) was also known as the Irish Giant prior to Patrick taking the title, it was said that he owed his great height of 7 feet 7inches because he had been concieved on the top of a haystack ! Unfortuanatly he was was robbed of his lifes savings of about £700, took to drink and died aged just 22.

The Norfolk Giant

Standing at a declared height of 7 ft 7 inches, (when the average height was around 5 ft 4) Robert Hales the Norfolk Giant was another to exhibit himself during the 1840's. He apparently joined Barnhams 'freak' circus of curiosities in 1849 and married a fellow giant called Elizabeth Simpson, who was also from the circus. After his retirement from the shows he went on to run the Craven Head Tavern near Drury Lane in London. An establishment often frequented by actors of the time.

Robert Hales visited Leicester in 1846, where he met up and took a glass and pipe with old friends at the Bishops Blaise on Causeway Lane on old 18th century inn. He sang a few songs and finished the evening with a 'fantastic toe'. The Bishops Blaise closed in 1939 the license was transferred to the newly built Blue Moon on Carlisle Street.

Circa 1854, Drury Lane, Robert Hales the Norfolk Giant's Craven Head Tavern is the building on the left with the lamp, facing the Cock & Magpie on the right.

Tom Thumb

The great showman Phineas Barnham promoted the American Charles Stratton who was born in 1838 and had stopped growing at the height of 25 inches. Barnham exhibited the midget around the world under the name of General Tom Thumb, named after an English folk law character. Tom Thumb's shows were extremely successful; he was even presented to President Lincoln and to Queen Victoria on three occasions. In 1859 General Tom Thumb visited Leicester appearing at the temperance hall.

An advertisement of the time read as follows;

Under the patronage of Her Majesty, the Royal Family and heads of Europe a rare combination of novelties. General Tom Thumb, the original and celebrated American. The little general will appear as sixteen characters, appearing with him is Picco the blind Sardinian minstrel and other rare novelties.

Following his success in Leicester, later that year a pub was named after him, situated at 21 Wharf Street. The Landlord Richard Farbarrow was often in the courts for one misdemeanour or another, culminating in a sentence of 9 months in prison for receiving stolen goods in 1865. His wife was also charged but was acquitted. The Tom Thumb pub seems not to have survived after that court case.

One incident at the Tom Thumb occurred in 1861 William Freer an old man was knocked down on the corner of the street by a funeral hearse carrying two coffins driven by Mr Ginns of the Fleur de lis. The Ginns family became well known later as partners in the well known firm of Ginns and Gutteridge funeral directors which are still trading today. The shaft of the cart had broken Freer's neck. He was carried into the nearby Tom Thumb pub in an insensible state where he died later that day. The inquests verdict was accidental death due to concussion of the brain by being run over by a funeral hearse.

Accidents by horse and carts were common, another fatality, this time involving a young boy occurred in 1841. Three boys on their way home from school, stood on the causeway outside the Cap & Stocking in East Gates, when a runaway horse and cart bolted down Silver Street at a furious rate, knocking down the three boys, the boys were carried in to the Cap & Stocking, young Billy Sharp was so dreadfully injured that within minutes he was dead, his skull badly fractured by the carts shaft. At the inquest a verdict of accidental death was recorded, the horse was found responsible and levied with a fine or deodand 'given to God' of £2. A deodand was levied when an animal was considered as the cause of death of a human.

Another to tour the country was Thomas Topham with his immense strength he would travel exhibiting his prowess. He appeared at the Three Crowns in Leicester with the Aldermen and Mayor in attendance, where he showed off his powers by bending a kitchen poker around his neck. Thomas continued by bending nails with his fingers and lifting a 6ft long oak table with his teeth, another of his feats was holding back a horse whilst another man was whipping the steed.

The Three Crowns on the corner of Horsefair Street and Gallowtree Gate, it was Leicester's major coaching Inn. The National Westminister bank now largely occupies the site.

Thomas Topham was challenged there by Leicester's strongest man, an altercation ensued, Topham picked up the man dunked him in the horse trough, carried him to the kitchen and hung him on a ceiling hook to dry!

Thomas managed a few years later to buy himself a pub in London with his savings (The Apple Tree) but he suffered an inglorious end. Returning home unexpectedly early one day in 1749 he found his wife 'entertaining' another man (wrong move) Tom went berserk and threw the other man down the street. He then turned on his wife, viciously attacking her with a knife before reportedly cutting his own throat. Miraculously his wife survived, Thomas didn't, she inherited his estate and continued running the tavern, now renamed as 'The Strong Man'.

The Elephant Man

Leicester's own Joseph Merrick often known as the 'Elephant Man'.

Mary Jane Potterton was born in Evington in 1836 she was the third child of William and Elizabeth. Mary married Joseph Rockley Merrick in December 1861 and their first child Joeseph Cary Merrick was born on the 5th of August 1862 . She was much loved by her son but she died at the early age of 36 in 1873.

Joseph, like Patrick O'Brien was modest and dignified, his deformity was of the worse kind, growths on his face giving him a most hideous appearance. Unable to support himself (he tried to hawk from door to door) Joseph was to spend part of his life in the Leicester Union Workhouse.

The Leicester Union Workhouse and staff circa 1870.

Later to become the Hillcrest Hospital situated on the corner of Swain Street and Upper Conduit Street - now renamed as Maidstone Road. Only some of the railings and exterior walls have remained intact after it's demolition in 1977.

Local publican and entrepreneur Sam Torr had recently left the Green Man in Wharf Street and opened the Gladstone Vaults with the 'Gaiety Palace of Varieties' Joseph was born close by in Lee Street and was well known in the area. He was first shown as a 'freak' by Torr in an opportunistic venture. Torr then set up a consortium of likeminded showman to tour Joseph around the country. Tom Norman exhibited Joseph in a shop in Whitechapel until the police closed it down. From here Joseph was taken to the nearby London Hospital under the wing of surgeon Frederick Treves.

Much has been written on Joseph Merrick and a moving portrayal by John Hurt in the film The Elephant man tells his story. In his later years he was feted by society, even royalty came calling and when Princess Alexandra presented him with a signed photograph Joseph became a celebrity

On his death an inquest was held in 1890 at the London Hospital by Mr Baxter, the body was identified by his nephew Charles Merrick a hair dresser of Church Gate, Leicester. He had by this time been in the hospital for four or five years and was aged 28. Mr Ashe the house surgeon was called to his room on 3.30 p.m. on Friday the 11th April and found him dead. Nurse Ireland, of the Blizzard Ward (what an utterly depressing name for a hospital ward! What chirpy names were the others called?) She saw him on Friday morning when he appeared to be in his usual health although he did not touch his midday meal. The coroner agreed with the doctor that the cause of death was asphyxia from the weight of the head pressing on the windpipe during natural sleep.

He remained humble, rarely complaining of his life of adversity. Joseph's head became so heavy he was unable to lay flat on the bed, he died in 1890 when he finally lay down, his head weight suffocating him. Frederick Treves wrote later that Joseph Merrick just wanted to lie down like ordinary people, ending a sad life.

One of the last photos of Joseph Merrick taken in 1889, shortly before his death.

Did you know?

As stated earlier Joseph Merrick's early years as an exhibit stemmed from a meeting with Sam Torr of the Green Man in Wharf Street who was to embark on a new venture nearby.

GOOD CHEER AT THE GREEN MAN

Look at this for a concert programme ! Master Mole (of the Mole Family), a musical mole nobody can catch ; Misses Clara and Annie Torr, melodious chips of the old block ; Messrs Newton and Haynes ; the genial chairman. Mr W. Spencer ; and your old friend Sam with a wallet of new songs.

N.B.- If you want poor music or bad beer, don't call on SAM TORR.

From Sam Torrs promotional advert for the Green Man.

Sam doing his famous character 'On The Back Of Daddy Oh'

Sam Torr, publican, actor and entrepreneur opened the Gladstone Vaults as the Gaiety Palace of Varieties about 1883. He took Joseph Merrick from the workhouse to show him as a 'freak', but it eventually offered Joseph a living he would otherwise had never achieved.

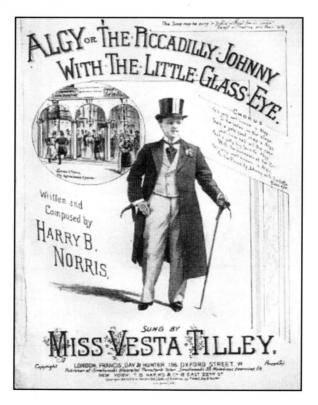

The Opening night at the 'Gladstone'

Top of the bill was Miss Vesta Tilly known as the greatest male impersonator. Later she was instrumental in encouraging soldiers to enlist in the First World War, portrayed as 'The Girl who loves a Soldier'. She once appeared on the back of a lorry in Leicester Town Hall Square aiding enlistment.

The top floor of The Gladstone during demolition.

The building in the 1990's minus the top floor, it was occupied by
G.E. Motor Factors for many years.

Daniel Lambert (1770-1809).

Leicester's most famous son a gaoler and 'heaviest man in the world' weighing in at a reputed 52 stone. Daniel was the 'turnkey' at the Leicester Gaol during the later part of the 18th century, Prisoners told of his affable nature and kindness. The Town Gaol was licensed to sell and brewed it's own ale, making it one of the most unusual outlets for alcohol. Daniel in fact claimed he was teetotal; he had followed his father as keeper of Leicester Gaol from c1788-1805 when the gaols amalgamated, Daniel found himself without a job and he made the decision to exhibit himself in London. He became the most fashionable person for those with money to meet and returned to Leicester a much richer man. Known for his sporting prowess, he could swim with two men sitting on him, he liked cock fighting and once was known to knock down a dancing bear when it attacked his dog. His terrier dog was his lifetime companion and he turned down extortionate offers of money to part with it.

Daniel Lambert with one of the pubs named after him, this one stood on the corner of Albion Street and Dover Street.

So fashionable and well known there was even a Daniel Lambert pub in London on Ludgate Hill, another is in Stamford where he died. Daniel was staying at The Wagon and Horses there on a visit to the races, the wall and window had to be demolished to extract his body, He is buried in the nearby St Martin's church yard, where his grave is still tended to this day.

Lenny Mason, Leicester Fat Boy

William Leonard Mason was born in Southgate Street in 1903. He is listed as one of five surviving children born to George and Clara Mason in the census return of 1911

Known as Lenny, he was described by the newspapers and magazines of the period as the fattest boy in the world. In America articles were written about the Leicester fat lad, one even suggested that he might become a famous film star. He was exhibited at several London fairs and died whilst staying at 112, Clifton Road, Finsbury.

He was aged only 16, his body, was returned to Leicester and it took eight men to carry his coffin from the hearse to his grave in the family plot at Welford Road Cemetery. He was buried on 7th of February 1920.

LENNY MASON, Leicester Fat Boy.

**Lenny posing for his photo proudly wearing a medal, presumably it was not won
for the egg and spoon race but possibly for being fat?
Lenny was said to have weighed 30 stone when aged 16.**

Circus Curiosities

The freaks were not the only exhibits to pull in the crowds, as the cruel 'sports' pastimes had abated, animals from around the world were 'shown' in an effort to entertain the masses. The arrival of the circus to town drew large crowds. Joseph Merrick believed that his mother being frightened by an elephant whilst pregnant caused his disfigurements. Many of the animals were stabled at the yard at the rear of the Fish and Quart on Church Gate.

Elephants parade on Charles Street passing the jobcentre to the right of the picture.

Barry remembers being taken to Leicester by his father to see the parade.

The local press reported an incident of an elephant mistaking the low bonnet of a sports car for the large stool that they were trained to sit on in the circus ring, resulting in a seriously squashed bonnet.

Music Halls were also on the high agenda for entertainment. In 1862 Dan Cook advertised the 'Alhambra' Music Hall the first in Leicester, previously called Stevens New Circus housed in a large wooden building at the rear of the Fluer-de-Lis Belgrave Gate. The circus had a tragic ending when in 1861 Stevens son, a little boy of 14 whilst dressed as a monkey, climbed so high on a rope that his cotton hair caught fire from the gaslights, which resulted in an agonising death for the poor little soul.

The original Fluer-de-Lis on Belgrave Gate

During the 1930's a more modern and ornate façade was added to the building. The rear of the building was sold off to the Council in 1931 as part of the redevelopment and widening of Charles Street. In the 1860's Samuel Ginns who also ran a buriel club from the premises owned the pub. It was the forerunner of the long established Leicester firm of Ginns and Gutteridge the funeral directors. The night security staff at the Haymarket centre, which occupies the old site, are convinced that is subjected to ghostly hauntings to this day!

Did you know?

It was common for the Corporation (of Leicester) to provide the preacher at St Martin's Church with a gallon of wine after the Sunday morning service to "comfort his inner man"!

Did you know?

In the reign of Henry VIII the daily diet allowed for a lady of the bed chamber by royal warrant, included a gallon of ale at breakfast, another at dinner, half a gallon of ale with a manchet (fine quality wheat bread, loaf or roll) in the afternoon. Followed by a gallon of ale and half a gallon of wine at supper!

Drunk in charge of the graveyard!

Many of those people who were of an usually large build or suffered deformity dreaded the thought of their bodies being stolen after death, some even requested to be buried at sea often to no avail as the medical profession would pay huge sums of money for rare examples.

The practice of robbing the graves of those who had recently died (body snatching) was carried out in Leicester, as the records of St Margaret's Church dating from February 1825 confirm. The relevant text reads as follows *"Notice is hereby given that a Vestry meeting will be held in the church on Thursday next at 10 o'clock to take into consideration the best mode of proceeding in order to discover and prosecute the person or persons who have lately stolen and taken away a corpse from the church yard and prevent such horrid practice. Also to take into consideration the general conduct of the Sexton, and the propriety of dismissing him from office"*.

There are no records of the culprits being caught, the unfortunate Sexton, Thomas Stringer was dismissed. Although not implicated in the grave robbing he was sacked for "Drunkenness and neglect of duty".

Due to the threat of having their bodies stolen many of the rich were buried in mort-safes, which were large heavily built tombs. For added protection they often had walls or gated fences surrounding them, examples of these can still be seen in many Leicester churchyards.

Saint Margaret's Churchyard

The stolen bodies were taken for use in medical schools, and grave robbing was resorted to as the demand outstripped the only accepted supply of felons who had been executed. Amazingly it was at this time not a crime to steal someone's body, but you could be prosecuted for stealing the dead persons clothes. This sadly resulted in the deceased person being dug up and stripped naked prior to being sold!

The teeth of the deceased were removed as these could be sold separately to dentists for the construction of false teeth. Human teeth were in great demand and the term "Waterloo teeth", evolved from the teeth that had been plucked out of the dead on the battlefields in France, and they were then shipped back in barrel loads to England. Because these teeth were in good condition as they came from generally fit young men killed in action, they were highly desired and commanded a premium.

When an act was passed in 1832, (the Act For Regulating Schools of Anatomy) it effectively put an end to grave robbing, as the new law allowed the workhouses to become the major supplier of bodies to the medical profession. It was economically sound practice for them to sell or even give away any unclaimed bodies for dissection rather than the parish having to pay for burial costs.

6
Murders and Executions

William Gardiner, a Leicester hosiery manufacturer (1770-1853) records, in one of his published 'notes', of a brutal robbery carried out by three Irish soldiers upon Dr Alexander of Dannetts Hall, Leicester. Two of the perpetrators were sentenced to deportation, the third remained in custody, awaiting execution. He was incarcerated in the gaol in Highcross Street but two days prior to being hanged made his escape, scaling the prison wall and dropping down into the garden of an adjacent public house, The Shoulder of Mutton, which fronted High Street. A servant girl at the Shoulder of Mutton had gone-a-milking and had conveniently left the pub key under the doormat. The condemned man was able to enter the pub and escape into the High Street, still wearing prison chains and leg-irons. He made his way over North Bridge and took to the fields. Eventually, he came across a blacksmith who, obligingly, removed his leg-irons. Luckily for the escapee, the good folk of Leicester – some of whom he must have passed during this daring episode – either didn't care or realize he was a man on the run from the law but surely his chains and leg irons would have given them a clue?

A substantial reward was offered for his re-capture but he was never seen or heard of again.

The Shoulder of Mutton Public House on High Street, Leicester, which later became the Haunch of Venison and is currently known as the Orange Tree.

91

George Davenport, Leicester's notorious highwayman, frequented many of the town's pubs. An enthusiast of tavern life and a practiced thief, he stole, sold and spent his ill-gotten gains in many of the town's inns. On one occasion he purloined a silver tankard from the Blue Bell in Humberstone Gate and was later arrested at the White Horse in Gallowtree Gate. This tendency for stealing tankards was shared by a former landlord who had previously been hanged for the same offence.

Born in Wigston, George's "party piece" was to climb to the roof of the Crown Inn and perform an impromptu song and dance around the chimney. Over time, he became an infamous character, feeding his lavish spending habits. He took to petty crime, foot padding (robbery on foot) and highway robbery. He often frequented the Woolpack (now Swatlands Indian Restaurant) in Oadby, only a short distance by horse and where many of his earlier crimes had taken place.

One narrow escape by George is recorded in Lloyd's Evening Post of March 1794:

On Saturday night laft, about eight o'clock, as Mr. Thoineloe was returning from Leicefter market, he was attacked upon the Narborough Road by two footpads, one of whom he knocked down with his ftick, and fome perfons fortunately coming up at the moment, fecured him ; the other efcaped. Wm. Lawson, the perfon in cuftody, has impeached his accomplice George Davenport, of Great Wigfton, who has abfconded.

At around twenty years of age, he enlisted in the Leicestershire Militia and was promoted to corporal but was court marshaled and discharged because of a neglect of night duties due to his "addiction to women and stealing from soldiers and sailors". He joined the army on a number of occasions, pocketing the King's Shilling and promptly deserting. As a wanted man, therefore, he needed to keep on the move although, whilst lodging in Loughborough in March 1783, he managed to find the time to court and marry a local girl Elizabeth Greendale. To evade capture for prior misdemeanours, he fled to London and found lodgings at the Green Man & Still, close to St Paul's Cathedral and which (somewhat predictably) was also the hive of local thieving fraternity. It is not known how George faired or how long he stayed in the capital but the homing instincts in him eventually returned him to the bosom of his family and his Leicester drinking buddies. Neither was it long before he recklessly undertook to hold up the landlord of yet another pub, the White Bear.

Strange to relate, it was for a comparatively minor offence that George was eventually arrested - poaching. At which point, he provided a false name but was, nevertheless, carted off and charged, as he either could not or would not pay the necessary fine. He was remanded in custody, therefore, which proved to be his undoing for on his short journey from the courthouse to the gaol and still handcuffed to the Peace Officer, the two decided to drop into the Saracens Head for a swift pint. (Such a thing is hard to credit these days, an Officer of the Law calling at a public house for a drink with a criminal attached to his wrist). And it was at this point that George's true identity was finally revealed - much to the astonishment of the Peace Officer who couldn't believe his luck! As a result of this disclosure, poor George was tried for all his previous offences, including a robbery from the landlord of another pub at Kegworth.

Thus it was that George Davenport, a renegade son of an otherwise well-connected Leicester family, was tried, subsequently found guilty and sentenced to death. He was taken to Red Hill, near Birstall, where he was hanged.

> *George Davenport, convicted at the late assizes at Leicester of a highway robbery, was thirty-nine years of age, eighteen of which he had, according to his own confession, been a highway robber. He had deserted from different regiments forty times, and had frequently escaped from gaol. He has made some important discoveries. He went from the prison to the place of execution, in a post-chaise, accompanied by his brother, and dressed in his shroud, &c.*

Extract from the Monthly Mirror of 1797

**One of George Davenport's many haunts, the Bell Hotel, in Humberstone Gate,
known during George's time as The Blue Bell public house.**

As previously mentioned, George had stolen a silver tankard from the Blue Bell and prior to his execution the landlord, John Douglas, was himself condemned for highway robbery. He suffered the same fate but failed to attain the same degree of notoriety as the popular George Davenport.

The Talbot pub

This was the last stop of the journey for many condemned prisoners on their way to execution. They often enjoyed their last meal at the Talbot before "entering into eternity" at the Red Hill gallows.

The gallows

John Douglas took over as landlord of The Bell after he courted and married the landlord's daughter upon the death of her father. Running the business to a high standard, he gained many influential friends and acquired a reputation for kindness and honesty. Unfortunately, and by a strange coincidence, Douglas fell foul of the law when prisoners at Coventry Goal suddenly implicated him in past misdemeanours.

It was revealed that Douglas had previously escaped transportation in 1757 after having been convicted for the theft of a silver tankard. He was taken into custody and tried at the Leicester assizes. The sentence of the Court was death by hanging. There followed a short reprieve due to petitions from the Mayor, Alderman and Councillors, whose fulsome praise described Douglas as a 'respectable' and 'model citizen'. The petitions were in vain, however, and Douglas was hanged for returning from transportation before his decreed term of banishment had fully expired.

By the end of the 18th century the Bell had become one of Leicester's major coaching Inns. The fare to London, seated inside the coach, was £1.0s.8d.. Outside 14/-d. (only 70 pence in today's money) and was guaranteed to arrive at The Swan with Two Necks in Lad Lane, London, the following day.

The Swan with Two Necks, Lad Lane, London.

A coaching token depicting, speed, regularity and security

Did you know?

The Cherry Tree in Bond Street was the recruiting centre for the Leicester Militia Regiment. Sometimes amnesties were held there and deserters from the army could surrender without incurring severe punishment. George Davenport took advantage of this offer and surrendered to the Guards Regiment but, true to form, he swiftly re-enlisted and absconded.

Murder at The Blue Boar

The story of King Richard's stay in Leicester prior to his defeat at the Battle of Bosworth is well known. His belongings and valuables, including his bed, were apparently left at the Inn. In the 1560s Thomas Clarke, the landlord, discovered the King's treasure hidden in a false bottom within the bed. As a result, Mr Clarke became rich and was eventually appointed Mayor. On his death in 1603, his estate passed to his widow, who continued running the Blue Boar. Her servants heard rumours of this treasure and one of the maids, Alice Grimbold, revealed her suspicions, under duress, to some male guests lodging at the inn. These men, led by Edward Bradshaw and Thomas Harrison, began ransacking the inn, searching for the treasure. Mrs Clarke endeavoured to cry for help but was, allegedly, choked to death by Alice Grimbold who forced her fingers down Mrs Clarke's throat – an act which Alice vigorously denied. Alice's accomplices then tied her up and fled, leaving her abandoned and stuffed into a chimney.

At the Assizes Court in 1606, records show that Edward Bradshaw had been convicted and executed for the murder of Mrs Clarke. The unfortunate maid, Alice, was burned at the stake.

The Blue Boar Inn

In 1831, King Richard's bed was offered to the Corporation to be placed in a museum but the offer was turned down. A few years later the Blue Boar was demolished and the large bed was cut up and removed to a house in Redcross Street.

Did you know?

The Beer Act of 1830 stipulated that for the cost of a two guinea licence fee anyone could sell ale. Within two weeks Sidney Smith wrote: "Everybody is drunk, those who are not singing are sprawling".

Peppermint Billy

William Brown (known as 'Peppermint Billy' because his father manufactured peppermints) was a Leicestershire lad who, at the age of nineteen, was sentenced to ten years' transportation for theft in the year 1843. It is not apparent what he stole - although silver tankards were a popular choice (!). He served his full sentence in Australia, but returned to Leicester bitter man.

Three years after his return to England, he absconded with his sister-in-law, who was living with her husband in Bedford Street. Threatening to shoot anyone who tried to intervene, he made off with her towards Melton where, at the Thorpe Tollgate, Brown shot and stabbed the tollgate keeper, slitting his grandson's throat. Brown fled the scene and headed towards Wetherby in Yorkshire in order to evade capture. He attended a service at the Methodist chapel on the Sunday evening and, not being strictest adherent of religion; had followed this up with a visit to a local pub. It was then that the Hand of Fate struck. The pub's landlord had recently read a description of Brown published in a newspaper. He promptly detained him and summoned the police.

William Brown, also known as 'Peppermint Billy', wanted for the brutal murder of Edward Woodcock, Tollkeeper and his grandson on 19th June 1856.

(From a wanted poster of the time)

At the Leicester Assizes Peppermint Billy faced trial for the two murders, was found guilty and sentenced to death. He appeared somewhat relaxed about his fate and in order to emphasize the seriousness of this crime and his impending execution he was taken to see his burial place. Billy's reaction, however, was not what was expected and he simply stated " Ah! It's a nice place, aint it? I shall like to lie under the trees" Billy asked his father to attend his hanging and " to come and see him turned off ".

William Brown would have faced the gallows erected outside the Welford Road Prison. Public hangings were a common sight on temporary scaffolds and patients from the Infirmary were able to watch the event from their windows. Another vantage point would have been the Turk's Head, which was opposite the prison, on the Welford Road.

Welford Road Prison circa 1906

The Turk's Head

The Turk's Head provided the best seats from which to view public hangings when an estimated crowd of 25,000 people would turn up for the event. The modern term of `gala day` derives from `gallows day` when the pubs would open early, often providing breakfasts and do a roaring trade selling alcohol to the assembled masses. Peppermint Billy's father watched his sons demise from the comfort of the Turk's Head. He was reputed to have observed, after his son was hanged: 'Well done Billy thou died like a brick'

The Turks Head was demolished around 1970 to allow for the expansion of the Royal Infirmary and its' new car park.

Incidentally, Leicester City player and Manager, Johnny Duncan, who had taken Leicester City football club to their first F.A. Cup final at Wembley in 1949 - and lost – later became the landlord of the pub.

Unlucky Valentine

Thomas Bloxham had been married for twenty years and together with his wife, Ann, had fathered eleven children when he began to convince himself that his wife was being un-faithful. After a prolonged drinking bout in a local pub, Thomas confided to friends that he was "going to kill her for it".

A crime magazine reported his trial:

> *"Such was the turmoil in his head and the constant rows with Ann, that Thomas went out and bought a revolver, fired it at his wife but missed, he then reached for a knife and severely cut her throat almost severing her head in his anger. Full of remorse he then turned the gun on himself, this time the gun misfired. At which point Thomas gave up and sent for the police".*

At his trial, Bloxham claimed that the whole business had been a 'suicide pact' and that when Ann had failed to stab herself to death he'd completed the job for her. The jury upon hearing all of the medical evidence did not even bother to retire. They had no trouble in finding him guilty and he was hanged at Leicester prison on Valentine's Day 1887.

Thomas Bloxham's local pub, the Mill Lane Tavern.
He and his wife lived around the corner in Fairfax Street.

All Saints' Brewery and a murder most 'orrible

All Saints' Brewery was established on Highcross Street in about 1790. Over the years, various families were involved in running the business and during its history it was passed from father to son and, on occasions, through marriage. Some of the early owners and partners in the brewery originated from London and the Home Counties, where the practice of brewing large amounts of ale at a central location and selling it through their own retail outlets was a long established practice. By contrast, Leicester had many family-run pubs brewing small amounts of their own beer. It was a good opportunity, therefore, for Southern based brewers to purchase or lease premises at extremely competitive prices compared to those in London. They could then establish large capacity local breweries, selling their products through acquired public houses. This was the origin of the later vast pub chains

Some of the remaining brewery buildings circa 1990.

John Wills Goodwin, Thomas Godfrey Cock, Frederick Graves Moon and William Langmore were all, at one time or another, partners in the brewery and all originated from London.

Frederick Graves Moon was a son of Sir Francis Graham Moon, 1st Baronet of Portman Square. Sir Francis, a successful printer and publisher by trade, was appointed as Lord Mayor of London in 1854. He died in October 1871. Frederick died a little before his father on 24th May 1871. The cause of Frederick's death - a poultry knife with a seven-inch blade which had been thrust into his chest — proved a public sensation and was reported in The Times.

The Bayswater Mystery

At the time of his death, Frederick Moon was a bachelor aged 41. He was a wealthy man with an annual income of £3000. Although a brewer by trade, he was never seen to be the worse for drink. He was not a sporting man neither did he indulge in betting. He appeared generally happy with life, although he does appear to have had a strained and erratic relationship with a lady named Flora Davy, who he had known for about twelve years. It was an obsessive and volatile relationship, punctuated by periods where there was little or no contact between them.

Flora operated under a number of names including those of Mrs Frances Canning, Madame de Morne, Flora Canning and Flora Newington. In fact her real name was Hannah Newington. She had no regular income and had been declared Bankrupt shortly prior to Frederick's death. On that particular evening, Flora was tracked down to a house in Bayswater which she shared with a one Mr Davey but to whom she was in no way related and charged with Frederick's murder.

Flora was not married to the Mr Davy who owned the lease of the house on Newton Street. However, he did stand surety for her bail following her arrest on the night of the stabbing. (The police wrongly assumed him to be her husband because she was arrested under the name of Mrs Flora Davy).

The Times recorded a servant at the Bayswater house provided the following statement at the inquest regarding the day of the stabbing:

> "Mrs Davy was in good spirits. She had champagne for luncheon at about one o'clock. She was in the habit of taking brandy. Witness could not say if she took brandy on Wednesday. She had seen her very much excited, but could not say if it was in consequence of what she had taken. There was some Burgundy on the table."

Flora had been under the care of a Dr. George Phillips, who stated that she was accustomed to an excess of various stimulants. The doctor had ordered her to drink "a certain quantity of champagne" and, as a result, she had of late become more temperate in her habits. (One wonders whether resorting to stabbing might be a result of withdrawal symptoms caused by being prescribed her "champagne treatment").

The Times, Friday, 2nd June, 1871.

The Coroner then summed up the evidence, putting before the jury the three suppositions, which had been raised namely,

1. *That the deceased had committed suicide.*

2. *That he had fallen upon the knife by accident, either when the weapon was in his hand or in hers.*

3. *That she had, either fearing he was going to hurt her, or in a fit of passion, plunged the knife into him.*

It might become a question for the jury in the superior court to decide whether, being a habitual drunkard, she had, losing all power of self-control, committed the fatal act in a moment of temporary insanity, but this was not a question to be now considered. The attempt to show that she would be interested in his death had entirely failed, and all the evidence showed clearly that she repented almost as soon as she committed the deed, provided she did commit the deed.

The room was cleared, and the jury, after consulting together for about half an hour, returned a verdict of "Wilful murder against the person known as Flora Davy."

She was later tried and found guilty for the lesser charge of the manslaughter of Frederick Graves Moon in July of the same year at the Central Criminal Court in London. It was at the time a very high profile case and attracted much interest from both the press and the public. Flora was sentenced to eight years' penal servitude, at which point she fainted and had to be carried from the dock.

In 1874 she was released on a ticket of leave, after spending most of her confinement in the infirmary of Woking prison and, afterward, a short period of incarceration at Millbank. She had served less than half of her sentence.

The early release of prisoners on licence began in the 1850's. Criminals were given sufficient money to get themselves home. Additionally, any money which they had earned whilst working in the prison system was given them on release and provided by postal order. Such postal orders were only cashable at a post office nearest to the released prisoner's home address and it was hoped this would prevent them from immediately spending it on alcohol. It often only delayed the process. One released convict was so drunk that when two constables were called to re-arrest him, he threatened to murder them both!

The Moon family Arms, the motto translates to `Keeping a calm mind`.

In Burke's Peerage and Baronetage of the 1990's, the 5th Baronet Sir Peter Wilfred Giles Graham Moon is listed as residing at Portman Square, London and (somewhat bizarrely) at The Red Lion, Bradenham, Buckinghamshire – presumably, his country address! He is also listed as Managing Director of the now defunct Riton Inns and a member of the British Association of Innkeepers. So, at least one member of the Moon family had retained an abiding interest in the licensed trade.

William Langmore took over the brewing at the All Saints Brewery Company. Frederick Moon was his uncle. Watts and Son were formally merged with Langmore and Bankart in 1890.

By 1892 the main business was listed as Watts and Son (All Saints' Brewery Co) wine and spirit merchants 32 High Street and 21 Silver Street. William was still listed as a Director in 1916. His son Francis Graham Langmore remained with the firm long after it was taken over by Ind Coope in the 1920's. The Moon family continued to hold shares in the company until it was completely liquidated in 1954.

The Earl of Cardigan

Santa Clause leaving Foundry Square to take up his place in the grotto at Lewis's department store in 1938.

St Mark's Church is on the right of the picture on the corner of Foundry Lane; the Earl of Cardigan public house is to the left. At the end of the Foundry Lane can be seen the building occupied for many years by Cort & Co iron foundry after which the area was named. The foundry was established in 1799 by James Cort and later became known as the Cort and Bell Britannia Iron works. It was at that time Leicester's principle iron works and sited for easy access to the Grand Union canal and wharfs.

The pub was named the Foundry Arms in 1815. A beer house with the same name was later opened close by at 174 Belgrave Gate but the pub had already been renamed The Waterworks Tavern. The beer house was also an eating house run by Joseph Brown and his wife in 1846. Joseph was also a carpenter. As was often the case with small beer houses, there was insufficient income to support an entire family and so additional trades needed to be undertaken. Another pub called the Iron Founders Arms on Belgrave Gate gives another indication of the impact Corts had on the locality.

The Waterworks Tavern was sold at auction on the 12th March 1854. It later The Cardigan Arms, then The Lord Cardigan and by 1877 it was known as The Earl of Cardigan. It stood next door to Central Motors but the building was demolished in 1958 and absorbed into the garage's own showrooms. The premises had survived as a pub for well over one hundred years, finally closing in August 1941. As it had been situated in an area of the town known for its slum housing, overcrowding and high crime rate the pub was not the most respectable of places to visit. The Leicester Brewing and Maltings Company Limited, who had previously leased the pub since 1899, eventually purchased the premises in 1917 for a sum of £3,000.

Charlie Knight re-opened the building as The Cardigan Café, on the condition that he could feed and provide overnight accommodation for soldiers in transit from the nearby railway station. It was renamed The Blinkin' Owl, was subsequently raided by the police in 1957 and closed down soon after. Bill Aklvey, the owner a that time, went on to run the Derwent Lodging House on Wharf Street.

The Belgrave Gate area of the town was considered to be the worst part of Leicester. The population of the area swelled in the 1840s when Irish immigrants and migrant agricultural workers occupied houses around the Abbey Gate area. Joseph Dare wrote about a "one room up and one down" dwelling house that was normally occupied by an Irish husband, his wife, and six children which would have an additional ten or twelve men lodging in it at harvest time. Dare, when recounting the scenes in the district on a Saturday night had "Frequently seen a horde of drunken savages burst forth from their drinking to wind up the night with a fight, men shouting, women screaming, half-starved children crying and the whole of the assembly mingling their voices in blasphemy". Sunday evenings were apparently nearly as bad. A local woman stated:

> "I dread Sundays; there is such drunkenness and fighting, it is more like a village wake than the Lord's Day". The land in this area is low lying and for many years was susceptible to flooding. The fall of the ground alone was insufficient to allow for effective sanitation. The drains were often blocked up depositing raw sewage in the streets and houses.

A Royal Commission reported that for the period 1840-42 the average age life expectancy in those poorly drained areas of the town was just a little over 16 years of age. One visitor to this area observed "Numerous small, dark and dirty streets with their miserable huts and pestiferous atmosphere". The district contained back-to-back houses and some people even lived in converted pigsties, until these were condemned in 1855.

The Vicar of the nearby St Mark's Church, Canon Donaldson wrote about the poor conditions which prevailed in the parish as late as 1910:

"In this parish there is represented all the tragedy and pathos, shame and horror of modern social conditions- infant mortality, child labour, under payment or sweating of men and women, decadence of physical life, consumption, premature death, and a general low vitality, together with an almost complete absence of beauty and a dire lack of the graciousness and glory of life".

Panel decorations at St Mark's Church painted by Eadie Reid in 1910 entitled: "The Triumph and Apotheosis of Labour". Reid used local residents as models for his figures. The church, closed for many years, has re-opened as function venue. Happily, the panel paintings were preserved and can still be seen today.

References to The Earl of Cardigan public house feature prominently in the case of the murder of Nancy 'Annie' Jennings in 1912. Annie, a forty-nine year old prostitute, was a regular customer at the pub and also frequented the Crown & Cushion at 75, Belgrave Gate. She had been to The Earl of Cardigan at lunchtime for a tuppenny shot of whisky and had bought a shillings worth of rum "to take out". (You would have got a fair drop of rum for a shilling at that time, however in earlier years you could, quite literally, by a bucket of gin for the same amount)! Annie was last seen alive later in the pub at about eight o'clock on the evening of 2nd of January 1912. She purchased some beer and whisky also to take out and had told the barmaid she had a client staying overnight. Her almost naked body was found early the next day at her rented house nearby in a small court off Archdeacon Lane. There were signs of a fight having taken place but her throat had been cut. One Archie Johnson was arrested for her murder but found not guilty at his trial and was duly acquitted. No one else was ever charged with Annie's murder. Sadly, these random acts were, indeed still are, quite a common occurrence in destitute areas.

Prior to being re-opened as a café, The Earl of Cardigan was used as the local headquarters of the British Fascist movement. On 23rd May 1940, Oswald Mosley who had continued his 'peace' campaign was interned under Defence Regulation 18B, along with the most active of British fascists. His wife, the former Lady Diana Mitford, was interned also shortly after the birth of their son Max (who was eventually associated with Formula 1 motor racing. They Mosleys lived out the war together in a house in the grounds of Holloway prison. After the war, Oswald formed the Union Movement. Workmen who were converting the building in the 1940's found a quantity of abandoned literature promoting the movement.

Sir Oswald Ernest Mosley, Founder of the British Union of Fascists.

Did you know?

After any unexplained death an inquest would be held. This would often be held in a public house close to the incident. After the jury was selected the members of the court would all adjourn to the place where the body was discovered. The corpse would still be there as it was not moved until after it was viewed. Happily the inquest was held fairly promptly after the event although if the body had lain un-discovered for some time this would have been an even more dreadful experience. In the 17-1800's the Coroner was appointed for two years and was chosen from the members of the Town Council. There was no requirement for them to have any medical knowledge and indeed many of them were publicans as Leicester had an unusually large proportion of them serving as both Councillors and Aldermen.

Did you know?

In 1766 Thomas Bunney was sentenced to be whipped for stealing a great coat from the 3 Cranes in Gallowtree Gate.

Did you know?

In 1869 a census of the Town showed 16 Churches, 48 Chapels and 545 public houses. In addition it recorded that there were still more than 1,000 houses, which had no back doors or windows. In 1878 for every 1,000 children born 203 died in their first year, these figures continued to rise and by 1891 on average three babies were being buried every day of the year. The responsibility for this high level of infant mortality was largely apportioned by the British Medical Journal to the mothers in Leicester who were accused of ignorance and wilful neglect of human life. They were also criticised for feeding their babies a diet of "toasted cheese and whisky"!

James Cook and The Flying Horse

The Flying Horse was originally a beer house established circa 1831 situated on Wellington Street, it became a fully licensed public house and was known in later years as the Old Flying Horse.

The Old Flying Horse on Wellington Street, now the site of the Council office block numbered as 22-30 and called Wellington House.

In 1832 the beer house was being run by Mr Noakes, the house next door was owned by Mr Sawbridge and at the bottom of his yard was a stable with a small work unit situated above it. James Cook, who traded as a bookbinder, rented the building, it became the scene of a horrific murder.

108

THE LEICESTER MURDER.

We give the above sketch of the Workshop, and subjoin a ground plan of the Premises, where, in the broad light of day, the respected head of a happy family fell beneath the hand of a young, but deliberate and cold-blooded homicide, who, during the silent hour of midnight, brutally mangled his innocent victim, and gave his severed body to the flames, watching, with hellish anxiety, the progress of his revolting work of destruction.

Stable with Loft above.	Yard and Offices.	House.	Wellington-street.
	Bowling Alley.	Passage.	
Stable, with Shop above.	Yard and Offices.	House.	
		Passage.	

a Entrance to Mr. Sawbridge's house.
b Foot of the steps leading to Cook's shop.
c Door of the stable.
d Corner of the shop in which marks of blood were most evident, and where it had run through into the stable beneath.
e Cook's fire-place.

f Wall of separation, upon which the murderer was leaning on Thursday evening, and looking into the bowling-alley.
g Entrance to Nokes's house, the Flying-horse.
The out offices in Sawbridge's yard obstruct the view of Cook's shop from the back-window of the house.

The Yard is 18 yards long and 14½ feet wide.

Q   165

Plate 6. From *The Instructive Reader*, p. 165.

Mr Paas had travelled from London and was staying at The Stag and Pheasant Hotel on Humberstone gate. He had visited several bookbinders during the day in the hope of selling them equipment, tools and associated items. He was never seen leaving James Cooks premise. Cook had previously received tools from Mr Paas and some monies were still outstanding,. When Paas called to collect the debt he was struck on the back of his head by a binders press pin (an iron bar), he was robbed and his body dismembered to be burnt on the fire.

Whilst burning some parts of Mr Paas, Cook was next door at the pub, having a few beers and playing bowls and skittles in the rear yard. He appeared rather anxious apparently often looking up at the smoking chimney of his workplace.

Cook eventually went home to his house in the Wharf Street area, leaving a large section of Mr Paas body still burning away on his fire. Alarmed by the large amount of hot cinders emulating from the chimney, a strong smell and a bright light from the fireplace the police were called and Cook was duly returned to give an explanation. He stated that he had brought a large quantity of horsemeat for his dog, but did not like the look of it and rather than bury it he had decided to burn it instead. As the policeman had no proof of any wrong doing he was free to return home and his father promised to return him promptly the next morning in case any further action was to be taken.

Paas then 'did a runner' to Loughborough, where he stayed at the King's Head Hotel, before catching the stage coach to Manchester the next morning. From there it was a train journey to Liverpool and he could then find a boat bound for America.

A doctor had been summoned early the next morning after the burning flesh had been found and he identified it as being human. They also found two burnt thighs and part of one leg stuffed up the chimney.

Later many people thought that Cook had deliberately put a large section of the body on the fire in the hope that it would set fire to the building and completely destroy the evidence. The police then set about trying to find James Cook.

The inquest into the death was held on 6th June 1832 at the Dog and Gun pub on Market Street. Cook nearly got away but was finally arrested on a small boat in Liverpool whilst attempting to rendezvous with a ship to take him to America.

> " 7 o'Clock in the Morning, June 5.
> " Dear Sir,—Since writing to you we have taken the villain, after a very severe chase. He was making off in a boat near the Black Rock. We succeeded in running them ashore. Cook leaped overboard, and attempted to drown himself. When we secured him he took out a bottle, and tried to swallow something from it ; but Cummins knocked it out of his hand. We found 44 sovereigns, and a half guinea and 7s. 5d., about him, no notes, a silver watch, gold chain and seals, and a brooch. We shall be at Leicester to-morrow evening by the Red Rover. I find it impossible to get any other conveyance. I assure you it has been a very tight business, for I scarcely know what a bed is, and am now too happy to sleep.
> " I am, dear Sir, yours, &c.,

An extract from a letter reproduced in the Leicester Chronicle and later in The Times.

James Cook was hanged on 13th August at Welford Road prison an incredible estimated crowd of 30,000 watched his execution. His body was gibbeted and put on display at the corner of Aylestone Road and Saffron Lane where a further 20,000 people went to look at it. The assembled masses were so riotous and unruly the body was only displayed for three days before being taken down and buried nearby. It was the last occasion in Leicestershire that the gibbet was used.

The gibbet

The Green Dragon murder mystery

Following an argument over a wager on a game of billiards, between a Frenchman Francis Soules and James Fenton. Soules armed himself with a pistol and went to the Green Dragon where he was confronted by John Fenton the landlord and brother of James, an almighty row ensued, ending with

Soules shooting Fenton dead. The trial was held at the old Guildhall, Soules, much to the indignation of the Leicester public. was pardoned and released.. On John Fentons gravestone his epitaph was inscribed 'a sad example of the incompetency of the judicial institutions to punish a murderer'

A subsequent judgement ordered the gravestone to be taken down and destroyed, fortunately this was done and it still remains at the Leicester Cathedral.

The Angel

Considered as Leicester's foremost Inn during the 16th and 17th centuries, little remains of the inn although some parts can still be found off the Angel Gateway which connects Gallowtree Gate and the Market Place.

One of the few rooms left of the Angel still intact today

Royalty was entertained at the Angel, only the well connected were invited there including King Charles 1st slept at the inn a prisoner of the parliamentarians after the nearby battle of Naseby in 1645. The King after much procrastination was executed by axe some four years later.

The victorious Oliver Cromwell was entertained at the Angel. Mary Queen of Scots was commonly believed to have held here on way to her execution at Fortheringhay Castle in Northamptonshire on February 7th 1587. The executioner botched the first blow of the axe, the second severed her neck, and he finally finished off by using the axe as a saw to decapitate her head completely.

Mary Queen of Scots

Gaol Brewery

One odd fact relating to Inns Taverns and Alehouses is that Leicester Gaol also had a licence.

The Licence Justice records of 1728 show that the Leicester Gaol in Highcross Street had been granted a licence to sell beer. The gaol was privately run with a rental being paid to the corporation. The 'turnkey' or warder was able to raise money however he could. Selling ale provided two advantages, a good income and it also kept those inmates who could afford it in a drunken stupor. Money could buy many additional privileges and visitors as well as the prisoners were charged for any services. Daniel Lambert was the head turnkey from 1798-1805.

In 1825 the new prison was built on Welford Road, it operated under a harsher regime, the Governors' maxim was; *'If a man will not work neither shall he eat'*.

Following some concerns about the conditions in prisons and the treatment of prisoners a commission was set up in 1847. The crank system form of punishment was used for anyone sentenced to hard labour in Leicester. The crank handles were situated in the cells on the wall, with the main body of the machinery which included a revolution counter on the outside in the corridor. The crank handle had to be turned over 14,000 times a day by the inmates.

To enforce hard labour, deprivation of food was carried out, which meant that the prisoner had to turn the crank 1,800 times to earn breakfast, 4,500 for dinner, 5,400 for supper and 2,700 to complete the day. For those who would not, or could not complete the cranking, food was withdrawn resulting in prisoners going days without food. If that proved ineffectual, prisoners were confided in a small dark cell for three days and repeatedly punished by being whipped and flogged with the 'cat'.

Three Oadby prisoners were called before the commission, Isaac Weston, James (Ponto) Norman (Barry Lount's ancestor) and William Gilbert. Isaac Weston testified that he spent three months on the crank; *'as I was a strong man the governor would often tighten the weights so as to make it harder to turn, I lost several stone in weight, towards the end of my sentence my testicles hung so low I was forced to have them strapped up, the work was so hard I tried to break my arm on the machine'*.

James Norman told a similar story adding that he was so ill on release he *'kept to his bed for a month'* William Gilbert corroborated their evidence regarding the tightening of the weights which made it virtually impossible to turn.

The commission concluded that the Governor and warders were all guilty of cruelty, except one warder William Davenport (son of the notorious highwayman George) he escaped blame, the prisoners told of his kindness. They stated that the crank machine was a most severe and exhausting punishment and the withholding of food was illegal. This form of punishment was eventually stopped in 1852.

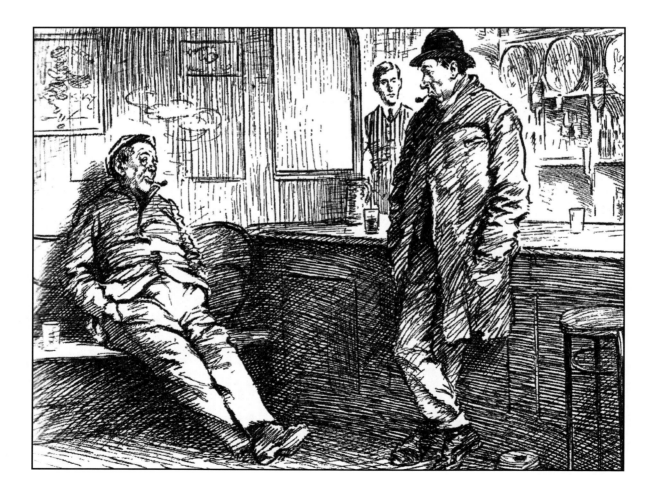

7
Strange 'appenings

Pubs, Inns and Taverns have a habit of being the home of many peculiar events.

Poisoned – can you smell a rat

Mrs Beswick was employed in 1899 at The Ropemakers Arms, situated on the corner of Taylor Street and Willow Bridge Street. One Saturday lunch time in February of that year, her husband George Beswick called into see her, he was complaining of feeling unwell. George told her he would fetch something. Later the same day George duly returned to the Ropemakers with a bottle containing a green powder, Mrs Wright, the landlady, asked where it was from and he replied that he had bought it from a nearby chemist.

The Ropemakers Arms around the time of the 'incident'

George Beswick started to mix the powder with water, much to the objection of witness's in the pub, who urged him not to drink the nasty smelling mixture, but unfortunately George did. He soon became unwell, started to twitch, eventually he went into a fit and dropped dead shortly afterwards. Richard Wright, the landlord, told the inquest that after Beswick had died in the pub he had found a bottle label in George's pocket titled 'vermin killer'.

Fred Willey a nearby Chemist told the Inquest that Beswick had called into his shop that Saturday afternoon to buy rat poison. Beswick had signed for it under the name of George Johnson. He also purchased some Laudanum (an opiate based mixture) at the same time. He confirmed that the vermin killer contained Strychnine, (medical examination had shown that he had died of Strychnine poisoning). Mrs Beswick told the coroner that her husband had not been well, finding it difficult to work. A verdict of suicide whilst temporarily insane was given.

Found one new born baby

Publicans find many strange things left in lavatories and cubicles, but Harris Rylott, landlord of the Royal Standard in Charles Street came across a most unusual find.

On the 22nd March 1887, Harris was called to the closet to find a newly born baby boy on the floor. He removed him, called for the police and a doctor, luckily the baby was still alive. Some regulars had recognised a woman called Catherine Jeffcot who had come into the pub's vaults with her daughter that day looking very ill and unsteady. She was given brandy and was last seen by them staggering about in the yard at the rear of the pub.

It transpired that Catherine was 26 years of age and the mother of a four-year-old girl. She had been widowed for two years and had been working at Baxter's in Lower Hill Street as a rag sorter for the previous five years. Catherine had worked that morning but had left at lunchtime saying that she felt unwell her state of mind that day is hard to imagine.

Catherine Jeffcot was remanded and charged with *'Abandonment of a child as to endanger its life'*. Although the baby was taken to the Union Workhouse he did survive the ordeal.

Seduction at The Stockdale Arms

Jasper Woodward and his family including a daughter Sarah, aged 17 ran a grocers and bakery in Albion Hill in 1874. Opposite was the Stockdale Arms run by William Pears, the two neighbours helped each other out in their businesses. On December 5th Sarah called at the Stockdale Arms with a delivery of bread, as she entered the kitchen Pears came in, he pushed her against the dresser and as Sarah described had 'connection' with her. Sarah reported later that *'I never knew anything of the kind before'*. The following January early one morning William Pears committed the same act on Sarah.

Subsequently Sarah found she was pregnant, when confronting Pears, he told her to take some steel pills and she would be all right, however in September her child was born. Sarah's father Jasper Woodward was extremely annoyed with the landlord of the Stockdale Arms and took him to court.

**Albion Hill circa 1950, The Stockdale Arms is on the extreme right
and the grocers shop is opposite.**

Pears was charged with seduction, with damages claimed for the inconvenience to Woodwards business through the loss of his daughters help, whilst she was carrying his baby.

At the court hearing Pears defence accused Sarah of having loose morals, indeed Pears had once said to her father; *'I am not the only one who has to do with your daughter'*. Witnesses were produced who admitted to *'entertaining'* Sarah. A servant girl at the Stockdale Arms claimed that Sarah had confided to her that she had been *'friendly'*, with a young man who was staying there. Even Sarah's sister thought the child was not Pears but another young mans.

When Sarah gave evidence she admitted being friendly with Harry Wright the son of the licensee at the Railway Hotel who apparently liked to look at her stockings as she had a *'good leg'* (sounds not un similar to Compo and Nora Batty). Sarah also admitted visiting the groom at the Railway.

The nearby Railway Hotel, at 20 Campbell Street, which Sarah would often visit.

Summing up, the barrister for Sarah's family claimed that liberal damages should be awarded. Not only for the suffering, sorrow and agony that William Pears had caused, but also for the damage to Sarah's character.

Pears defence argued that as no one could be sure who the father was, and with Sarah admitting to being *'light'* with other men she should be sent to a school of strict morals. After retiring the Jury returned with a verdict in William Pears favour.

The Swan and Rushes, death by lack of Brandy.

Keziah Bennett died aged 45 at the Swan and Rushes, 1 Infirmary Square in 1861. Because of her sudden and unexpected death she was buried by coroner's warrant on 5th June at Welford Road Cemetery.

SUDDEN DEATH.—On Monday an inquest was held in the parish of St. Mary, upon Keziah Bennett deceased. It appeared that she was 45 years of age, and the wife of Mr. S. Bennett, landlord of the Swan and Rushes, Infirmary-square. For the last six years she had led an intemperate life, and on Tuesday, Wednesday, Thursday, and Friday last week, was intoxicated, chiefly with brandy. On Friday afternoon she went to bed, and that night was better and more sober. On Saturday she was in bed most of the day, and had food taken her at various times, but nothing would remain on her stomach. Towards night she had some tea, and after 10 o'clock a small quantity of gruel; but about half-past 11 a person who was assisting in the house went up to her room, and found her apparently dead. Mr. Sidley was called in, and on examining her found that she had been dead from half-an-hour to an hour. He subsequently made a *post-mortem* examination of the body, and the result was that he attributed deceased's death to syncope or faintness, brought on by the sudden cessation of taking the quantity of stimulants to which she had been accustomed for the three or four days preceding her death, and to the stomach rejecting the food which she had tried to take. A verdict in accordance with the medical evidence was returned.

Tragedy at The Tailor's Arms

The Veasy's ran the Tailor's Arms on Colton Street during the 1880s, they had four children, two young sons and two daughters. Tragedy struck the family one evening. the two boys and a daughter Edith aged 7 had been put to bed. One of the boys was feeling ill, so a candle was provided in the bedroom Shortly after bedding down screams were heard coming from the bedroom. The eldest sister, who was still downstairs, rushed up to find the bedroom on fire with the two boys having scrambled to safety on the landing, but poor Edith was still in bed and surrounded by flames. Mr Veasy bravely dashed into the bedroom to rescue his daughter, in doing so he received severe burns to his face and hands. Mark Porter, a chimney sweep by trade, was in the bar and helped to extinguish the flames.

Young Edith and her father were both taken to hospital, she was still alive but severely burnt, sadly she died two days later. At the inquest, the two boys gave evidence that Edith had moved the lighted candle nearer to her bed moments before the fire had started.

Did you know?

Wm Thompson a militia man billeted at the Tailors Arms was given six weeks hard labour for stealing a pencil case from there.

A case of severe wife beating

Wife beating was a relatively common occurrence during Victorian times, even when it was severe enough to be considered as a crime it often carried a far lighter punishment than theft or poaching. The Jolly Angler in Wharf Street was where one particular case of wife beating reached a tragic conclusion.

Edward Everitt was the landlord in 1866. he and his wife Lydia ran the pub along with George Green who was the resident brewer. Edward and his wife Lydia were both described as being addicted to drink and were often 'addled'. Lydia perhaps became more of an inebriate after losing children in infancy and recently having miscarriages. Witnesses in the pub testified that on the last occasion Edward had hit his wife several times after they had had a quarrel behind the bar. She was thumped viciously to the head and eyes; he had also pulled out some of her hair and threatened to kill her. Lydia was then helped by some customers to a seat in the bar with her hair dishevelled and one eye hanging out. She was described as quite insensible, could not speak and was foaming at the mouth. Eventually she was carried upstairs to bed.

At six o'clock the next morning Lydia was found dead at the bottom of the stairs. Was she pushed? or did the beatings and drink render her senseless and she fell accidentally?

The coroner on hearing evidence from the regulars including the brewer George Green, concluded that Lydia had endured many beatings and that they had ultimately resulted in her demise. He announced his verdict of manslaughter against Everitt.

Everitt was tried on February 28th 1866 at the Guildhall of the lesser charge of common assault, for which he received a paltry twelve-month prison sentence.

'Shocking Depravity'

This was the headline in the case bought against Elizabeth Goddard, dubbed as the 'Wise women of Wharf Street' by the local press, it was both appalling and tragic.

In 1860, William Kellam and his wife Sarah were running the Princess Charlotte public house in Oxford Street. They had been married for about 20 years and had had nine children. The marriage was a troubled one, on more than one occasion Sarah had left her husband and had taken off with other men. In 1860 Sarah, who was still aged only 37, moved out yet again to embark on a relationship with John Harrison. William Kellam left the Princess Charlotte shortly after this and moved around the corner to Chancery Lane, continuing his profession there as a Maltster.

The Princess Charlotte on the corner of Oxford Street and the Newark, prior to the alterations. William and Sarah Kellam were the publicans here for three years until 1860 Sarah soon found herself pregnant again, living in what could be best described as a hovel in the Full Moon Yard just of East Bond Street. Sarah's shame, living conditions and circumstances forced her to search a way out of her predicament.

The previous year she had been to have her fortune told by Elizabeth Goddard, *'the wise women of Wharf Street'*, on that occasion Elizabeth had told Sarah that if she was ever in trouble she could help her get out of it. As a result of this previous meeting Sarah with one of her elder daughters Sophia, visited Goddard at her house in Wharf Street, confiding in her that she was "in the family way". Goddard replied "never mind I can take care of it, but it will cost you £1" and continued, "tell no one, when you have the money come to my house one night after dark"

Sarah trusted Goddard, (she was a midwife) and arranged to call the next night. Accompanied by John Harrison, they left Full Moon Yard and headed to Wharf Street, on approaching Goddard's house

Harrison parted from Sarah and went in the nearby Generous Briton beer house. Sarah carried on to Goddard's house. Within 20-30 minutes Sarah joined Harrison in the Generous Briton, they then made their way back to Full Moon Yard. It was about 2am that Sarah had what Harrison described as a "aguie fit" Sarah's daughter called the next morning to find her mother in much pain, Sophie called the surgeon Mr Crossley, he found Sarah in a sad state, describing her condition as desperate, laying in a wet and deplorable hovel, he thought she may have peritonitis and he would call the next day.

On Crossley's next call Sarah's condition had deteriorated, she was delirious, rambling and also shouting "Mrs Goddard has done the mischief, Goddard has killed me" he confirmed peritonitis and told her there was no hope. Shortly afterwards Sarah Kellam died with her daughter Sophia at her side. Later Elizabeth Goddard was arrested and charged with her murder.

Elizabeth Goddard was sent to the assizes for her trail before a packed courtroom in March 1861. Charles Crossley, a surgeon was called at the trial, his evidence was damming. His opinion was that peritonitis was the cause of death and had been caused by externally applied violence with blunt instruments. Elaborating he described Sarah Kellam as having three deep wounds, confirmed by post mortem, a punctured bowel and lining of the vagina, with her right ovary being completely destroyed.

Police Sergeant Wright testified, after Goddards arrest he searched her house in Wharf Street where he found a number of instruments which he produced to the jury. Having summed up the evidence the Judge directed the jury on their duty. They retired to consider the evidence, but returned after only half an hour to give a verdict of guilty to the charge of wilful murder on the defendant.

His Lordship donned the black cap, the courtroom fell silent as he addressed Elizabeth Goddard '*I have a duty to perform, that is that you will be taken from this place from whence you came and from there to the place of execution, that there you will hang by the neck till you are dead*'.

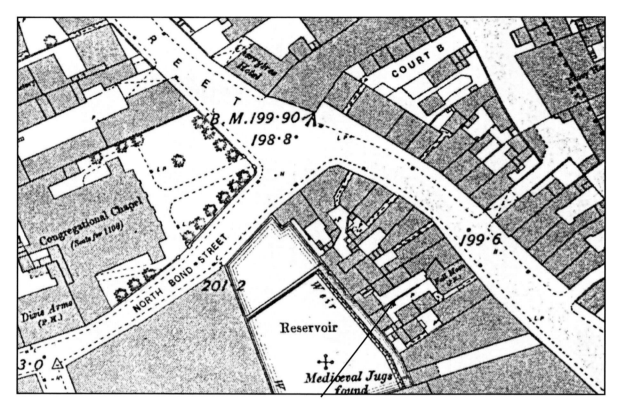

The Full Moon yard where Sarah died

Within weeks of Elizabeth Goddard's death sentence, an appeal was launched, there ust have last minute reprieve. The local headline read '*Respite received for wretched convict*'. Queen Victoria signed the conditional pardon, the amended sentence was firstly reported as transportation and later as penal servitude for life. It appears that she served only a relatively short period of incarceration as she is listed as a resident back with her husband Thomas, looking after an invalided niece at 140. Wharf Street by 1871.

Elizabeth died aged 64 in July 1878, she was still living in Wharf Street at the time of her death..

The tragic death of a landlord

A shocking tragedy behind the Blue Boar involved the landlord Joseph Tacey of the Gariboldi public house of 81 High Street. Mr Gregory ran a green grocery shop next to the Blue Boar; he also kept some cows in the shared rear yard. . Additionally he stored grain in an old six feet deep water cistern.

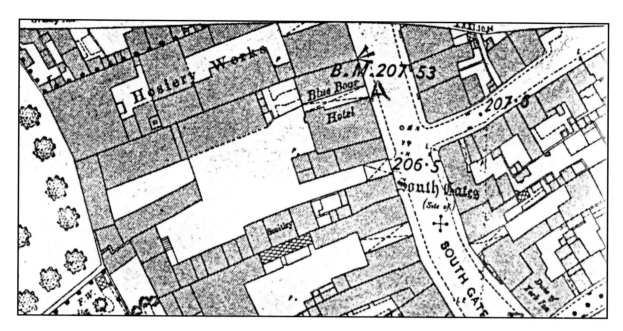

The Blue Boar, shared its yard with greengrocers, smithy and surrounding outbuildings, all were close to where the cistern was situated.

Gregory sent a young boy to fetch some grain from the store, but due to the awful stench the boy refused. Gregory who was rather obstinate, fetched a ladder, and lowered himself into the cistern, but was overcome by the fumes and dropped down in an insensible state to the bottom. Nearby Gregory's daughter Charlotte saw what had happened and attempted to rescue her father Charlotte was overcome by the obnoxious gases and fell down into the cistern on top of him. Joseph Tacey the landlord of the Gariboldi also worked as an ostler, he was helping to brush down some horses at the nearby blacksmiths in the yard. He and William Freeman both descended into the cistern to rescue Gregory and his poor daughter but Freeman, shortly followed by Tacey were both overcome by the fumes.

A fifth man Isaac Jackson, Freeman's brother in law was pulled back by William Faulkner, the landlord of the Blue Boar, fearing Isaac may sufferer the same fate. By now a few people had gathered in the yard to watch the drama unfold.

Four people now laid at the bottom of the cistern, Tacey seemed to be still alive but insensible. A nearby butcher brought some rope and hooks, by making a noose he was able to pull Tacey out, Unfortunately on reaching safety, Tacey was seen to roll his eyes and then he expired. The remaining three bodies were recovered and placed with Tacey in the stables. Four people died in the cistern due to the fermentation of the grain mixed with the water that caused carbonic acid and its gas to develop. If only Gregory had not been so obstinate and had listened to the young boys warnings it may not have ended in tragedy Collections were made for the unfortunate families the Tracey's received over £55. It appears that the pub closed shortly after this event.

A fatal twist of fate

Arthur Cain and his family ran the Empire Hotel on Fosse Road in 1926. A rather grand building it was originally built in the 1880s as a health spa where people could take the waters of the nearby Newfound pool. Captain Muir stayed here whilst arranging a display of parachute jumps from his aircraft at the nearby Blackbird Road flying ground.

Dorothy 'Dot' Cain, was by all accounts a vivacious woman, she was aged 25 and volunteered to do her first parachute jump.

The Leicester Mercury reported some 40,000 people turned out to witness the air display. The Captain and Dot took to the skies circling over the showground. Dot was given the signal, she climbed from her seat and took a plunge forward, the parachute sack caught on the side of the plane. She plummeted into thin air, watched in horror by her husband Arthur and family. Dot landed amongst the horrified spectators, hitting the ground with a terrible impact, which instantly killed her.

Dorothy was buried in Welford Road Cemetery, after thousands turned out to pay their respects as the cortège was routed from the pub to the cemetery. At the inquest Captain Muir insisted that he had fastened the harness clasp correctly, but it had somehow accidentally come undone.

Pub Names

The English and Welsh have always come up with inventive names for their pubs, mostly named after royalty, local landmarks, military hero's or battles and trade & profession names, a few more unusual ones which sometimes the reasoning is hard to fathom.

Uncle Tom's Cabin

After the publication of Harriet Beecher Stowe's best selling book in 1852 influencing opinion on slavery and the Deep South in America, Leicester had two pubs named after her novel. One in Stanley St built around that time as a directory of 1854 records the fact, another ad of the same year read; *In Stanley St, Humberstone Rd, all that newly erected Public House called Uncle Toms Cabin, with ample cellarage with gateway for the water, and well adapted brewery.*

Little is heard of this pub again it may have become the Stanley Arms that stood for around a century in this street. The other Uncle Toms Cabin was in Thames St, again in 1854, it became inadvertently involved in a strange case of some stolen water taps from the nearby Waterworks Co, which also had offices in Belvior St. A parcel of of 24 water taps was delivered to the office one Sat morning, left in a hamper at the gateway, shortly after they went missing. Abraham Markham was the suspect.

Markham together with another visited Uncle Toms Cabin on Sat lunch with a heavy sack in their possession, Markham was left alone whilst the other man went and fetched a third man named Faulkner, Faulker was then left alone with the sack, Markham and his companion left. Faulkner then asked landlord John Marston if he could leave the sack in the pub whilst he fetched a cart to carry off the sack in. The landlord became suspicious and on Faulkner's return asked him if he knew what was in the sack as he believed it contained stolen goods. Fulkner replied in the negative, said he was approached by a 'man in black' and another he did not know if he would go to Uncle Toms Cabin with his cart to carry some goods. andlord John Markham then fetched the police, who subsequently arrested Abraham Markham in the Newark.

Markham was charged and remanded, after investigations a second remand was ordered finely by he third court hearing, Faulkner seemed to have lost his memory of meeting Markham, Markham couldn't remember meeting Faulkner, nor sure if he was in Uncle Toms Cabin that lunch. e didn't know who the 'man in black' was 'the man in black' could not be found. In fact no one could remember anything anymore or how the sack of water taps came to be in the pub Much to the annoyance of the magistrates' they had little option but to dismiss the case, apart from the fact that 24 taps ended up in the pub, due to the confusion who knew what, who knew whom, who was the 'man in black' and the loss of memory by all. ever the less Markham was warned to his future conduct, leaving the court with a caution Uncle Toms Cabin later became The Gladstone Vaults.

The Pipe Makers Arms

The Pipe Makers Arms, St Saviours Road, was an unusual and extremely rare name for a pub. In 1878 Elizaberth Warburton ran an old-fashioned beer house and grocers from 71 St Saviours Road. Elizabeth and her husband Joseph had previously ran a clay pipe making business in George Street Leicester for nearly forty years until her husbands death. Pipe smoking was a fashionable and popular pastime often they were smoked whilst having a drink at the local pub. Pipes were made in various shapes and sizes and there were many makers in the town. Some were produced bearing the pubs name or logo and could be purchased from there. Briar pipes and cigarette smoking virtually replaced clay pipes, and the manufacturing of them had largely died out by the end of the First World War.

Elizabeth could not escape the scrutiny of local officials. in 1878 she was fined 10/- (50p) for selling bread otherwise than by weight

A butcher named Walter Gibbins prior to 1892 bought the house. it was subsequently purchased by another butcher Alfred Derry in 1929 and remained a butchers until its demolition in the early 1970's. The Pipe Makers was typical of many beer houses that later became off licences or corner shops combined with being general grocers.

The former Pipe Makers Arms taken about 1920

The Peeping Tom

Another extremely rare pub name was the Peeping Tom, on the corner of Gresham Street and Arlington Street in Leicester. It was a beer house in the 1870's, but did not last for long and transformed into an off licence and grocers. Luckily the name was never erased and survived until it's demolition circa 1970.

The Peeping Tom name can still clearly be seen above the sign.

The only other Peeping Toms that we can find were in Coventry and Warwick, deriving from the Lady Godiva legend of her riding naked on her horse through Coventry, all of its inhabitants turned away except Tom the tailor who supposedly was struck blind when he peeped as she rode passed. Hence Peeping Tom.

The Admiral Duncan

In 1868 The Tyler family ran the Admiral Duncan in Fleet Street to be followed by Silas Oakland some ten years later. Not long into his tenure he woke one morning to find that the pub had been broken into An extremely large quantity of property and stock were missing. This included a clock, over 40lbs of beef, a gallon of whisky, a shawl, sheets, three quarts of ginger brandy, some gin, brandy, three bottles of rum, 1lb of currents, 1lb black tea ½ lb green tea, 1lb raisins, 1lb tobacco and a box of cigars. The police suspected that the culprit new the premise and the approximate location of the various goods. The prime suspect was Arthur Tyler the son of the previous landlord.

Silas accompanied the police to Tylers House where he identified the clock and other goods as some of the property stolen from the pub. Tyler offered no explanation of how the items came into his possession. Arthur Tyler appeared at court, he was found guilty and received a nine months prison sentence with hard labour.

The Admiral Duncan

Many public houses were named after prominent Army and Navy senior officers, It brewed its own beer for many years and finally closed in 1907.

Halford Horatio Heich

One Leicester publican who had a colourful, eventful life and name was Halford Horatio Heich. He was a Leicester lad born in 1832 in Halford Street where his father ran a plumbing business. It is not recorded why Mr Heich named his son after Halford Street, Mr Heich may have named his child Halford to celebrate his place of birth and maybe his conception; sadly it is unlikely we will ever know which one.

The family decided to emigrate so in 1849 the business was put up for sale, shortly before embarking Halfords brother, William, died in unusual circumstances. He was suffering from a sore pimple (whereabouts unknown) and before going to bed one evening William covered the offending spot in candle (tallow) wax, a remedy often used to draw out the pus. During the night mortification set in and he was found dead in the morning. At the inquest it became apparent that some Chandlers mixed their wax with arsenic to improve the appearance of the candles. The coroner gave a warning (sadly a little too late for William) to the general public to be careful when applying candle wax to their bodies.

Halford joins the Unionists

The remaining members of the Heich family emigrated to America and settled in Ohio, Cincinnati. Halford was still in his teens when the American Civil War broke out but always up for a bit of a fight he gamely enlisted in the Army. The war ended in 1865, and Halford made his way back to Leicester with a substantial amount of money and gold, leaving most of the family behind in Ohio.

On his return, Halford advertised his services as an accountant from his lodgings based near a tripe shop in Humberstone Road. Within a few months Heich, together with his new girlfriend Fanny Marvin Wesley, were lodging in Wharf Street with the Mayo family. The gold and money were secreted in a tin, inside a wooden box and placed in a washstand under the bed. Halford had a habit of getting out the money playing with the notes with the Mayo children. Probably not the wisest thing to do, '*wait there kiddies just going to scramble under my bed, get my secret tin out and my wad of money so that we can play with it*', one suspects that Halford was not exactly the brightest berry on the tree.

Not surprisingly, Halford and Fanny returned to their lodgings one evening to find the gold missing. Suspicions soon fell on Mrs Mayo. Eventually, the gold was found buried in Mrs Mayo's sister's garden. Margaret Mayo was charged with the theft, found guilty and dispatched to prison for three months.

Halford returned to the States leaving behind a pregnant girlfriend and debts of over £300. He returned soon afterwards and married Fanny in 1867. In 1872 he and his wife were running the Crown and Thistle in Northgates.

The Crown and Thistle, prior to demolition on Northgate Street,
one of Halford Horatio and Fanny Marvin Heichs pubs in Leicester.

**Whites directory of 1877 with 'Horatio' at the Nelson
(and the Tyler family from the previous story at the Admiral Duncan).**

In 1874 they moved to the Admiral Nelson in Humberstone Gate an appropriately named pub for Halford **Horatio** Heich Five years later they again moved to the Reindeer Inn on Dunns Lane near the West Bridge, close to the West End Inn, by then they had a daughter Emma. Disaster struck the following year when Leicester and particularly the West End area was under siege from the Great Flood.

The Great Flood of 1881 in Leicester

In 1881 the river Soar broke its banks after torrential rain, Dunns Lane properties found themselves up to the window sills in water. The press reported that the inhabitants of Dunns Lane are in a *'deplorable condition'*.

Within a couple of months of the flood, Halford had gone from the Reindeer, a temporary licence was applied for to keep the pub open and Fanny finds herself moving to Outram Street with the children Frederick and Emma. Fanny describes herself as an *'out of work Publican'* A few weeks after the census was taken Fanny died aged just 35.

Another sad postscript is the suicide of the landlady of the nearby West End Inn who, through despair, threw herself off the bridge into the river, shortly after the flood.

Halford Horatio Heich seems to have totally disappeared.

8
Shorts and Snippets

The King's Head

The King's Head during the late 1990's, often known by locals as The Nut!

King Street was laid down in 1811-1813 shortly after the Corporation had acquired the surrounding land. This was part of the area previously known as South Fields that had provided free grazing rights for the freemen of the town. The Enclosure Award, ratified in 1811, gave the Council 453 acres of land and, in return, Freeman's Common was created close to Welford Road in an attempt to pacify local and often bitter dissent to the acquisition.

After the Act was passed, parcels of land were sold off to defray legal costs incurred by the Council. Much of the more desirable land close to the expanding town was quickly purchased by members of the Town Council at much reduced rates and either developed by them, or sold on at true market value, returning them a considerable profit.

The King' Head dates from about 1826, William Wragg was the first recorded landlord.

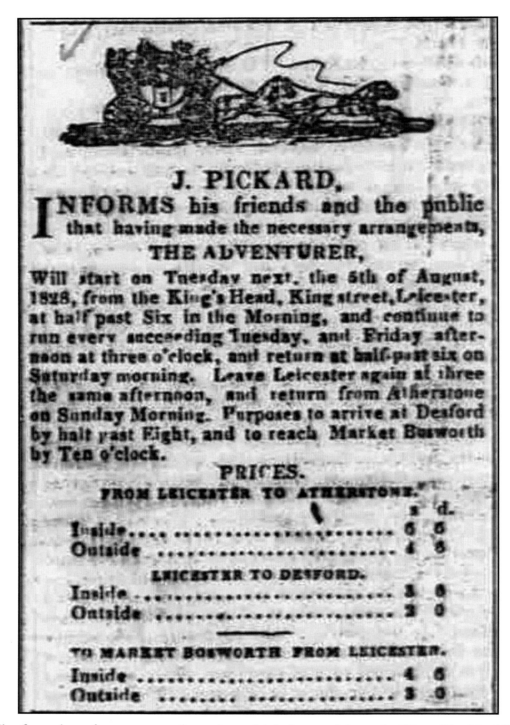

The first advert for a new coach service, which departed from the Kings Head in 1828

Thomas Foxon was the landlord of The Kings Head from about 1861- 1867 , he was also a brewer moved from there to manage the White Swan in the Market Place from about 1868. In 1861 he is recorded at the King's Head with his wife Caroline and their three daughters aged from 1 to 6. One son Ernest died there in December of 1863 at the age of 8 months and he also lost another child who was apparently still born in February of 1865. Tragically two further children, born later at the White Swan suffered the same fate in 1872 and 1874.

In March 1862 Thomas appeared in court when his brother, John was charged with receiving stolen boxes of cigars. Henry Greet who worked for a local cigar maker had stolen an amazing 81 lbs of cigars from his employer. John had 31 boxes of them at his house, nine 'cleverly' hidden under his bed. Thomas had purchased some of the cigars from his brother and sold them at the pub. Greet and John Foxon both received a sentence of twelve months imprisonment with hard labour, Thomas luckily managed to avoid any punishment.

Thomas Foxon went on to run The Anchor situated on the corner of Charles Street and Halford Street, he died there in 1892 aged 62. Thomas was also associated with other pubs including the British Lion on Russell Square.

The Clayton family ran the pub from at least 1868 until 1939. George Clayton the father started his working life as a clerk for the Midland Railway. He was relatively young for a landlord aged 24 in 1871 he was also the brewer. George also brewed at the Forester's for a time, which he may have owned for a relatively short period, but it was taken over by Charles Scotney in 1881.

ST. MARY'S LODGE, N.I.O.O.—The annual dinner of St. Mary's Lodge of the Nottingham Imperial Order of Oddfellows was held on Monday, at the King's Head Inn, King-street. Dr. Sloane, one of the medical advisers, presided, supported by P.P.G.M. Forknall. There were also present, P.D.M. Winterton, treasurer of the lodge; P.I.M. Clayton; acting C.M. Thorpe, from Manchester; P.P.G.M. Baxter, P.P.D.M. Bramley, P.P.D.M. Forknall, and P.G. David Berry. About 70 sat down to a well-cooked, plain, and substantial dinner.—After the cloth had been drawn and the preliminary toasts had been duly given and responded to, Mr. Clayton proposed "The Leicester Provincial Chapter and Officers of the Chapter," to which Mr. Johnson responded.—Mr. Johnson proposed "The Nottingham I.O.O. and Benevolent Institution," and explained the history of the Order.

A record of a friendly society annual dinner at the Kings Head, held on Monday 10th of June 1878.

George Clayton was the host for the event and was also a senior officer of the society.

Weaver's Bar

Weavers bar opened at 54 King Street in the late 1990's featuring former framework knitter's cottages. Cramant's Yard consists of a row of knitters cottages built circa 1826; tiny places with only one bedroom and one room downstairs, even so they often-housed large families. Thankfully, the buildings are preserved and were converted at that time to be used as intimate seating areas. The bar unfortunately did not last for long, however the premise is now occupied by a pre- school nursery.

The Little Crown

The Little Crown in the Market place had its licensee charged in 1872 of '*allowing persons of bad character to assemble in his house*', it was found that there were six women with four young men, three of whom had their arms around the women's necks and two had their legs crossed over the women's knees.

> **Drunkardness cured, even without the knowledge of the patient, the most certain and inexpensive cure, safe and perfectly harmless, given in a cup of tea or coffee, IT NEVER FAILS, it has cured and restored happiness to thousands of families, it cures cases of however long standing, to send for this remedy send 1/3d To Mr Deacon-Medical Botanist.**

From an advert in a Victorian Newspaper.

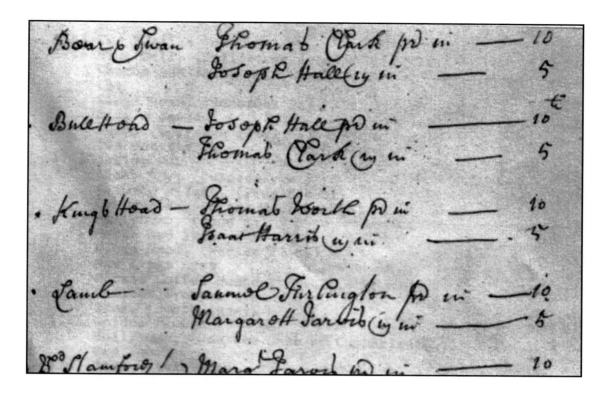

Part of the local authorities duties was to collect the license fees and also sureties in the form of a bond and record them accordingly. These are part of the document for 1735, an interesting feature emerges at the start of his journey around the alehouses the handwriting of the recording clerk starts off beautifully written (above). However by the time he had visited a dozen or so premises the handwriting had fallen into a hardly decipherable scrawl (below). The last entry on the page, relates to the Bath Coffee House and it certainly looks like he could do with a strong black one and a cold bath!

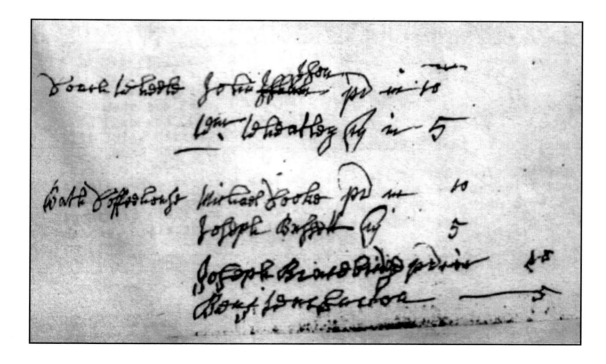

Terrible Accident at The Criterion

Gallowtree Gate was brought to a standstill when Fred Smithy, a cook 23 and Louise Durham 21, both fell over sixty feet to their deaths after leaning against the stone balustrade on the roof of the Criterion when part of the stonework gave way. It was fortunate that the falling debris injured no one else

Centre left. The restaurant roof part of which came away.

Some passers by saw the pair clutch each other on their fall as they turned a complete somersault. Mr Crowhurst the owner of the Criterion rushed out as a crowd gathered around the stricken pair. An ambulance was called but it was to late to save the unfortunate couple.

At the inquest July 1885, Mr Crowhurst informed the judge that the building had only been erected for about ten years and was built to the highest specification. The roof had never been intended for standing on, however staff would often spend time up there looking out on the town streets. Indeed fourteen people were on the roof to watch The Prince of Wales when he visited Leicester about three years ago. Examination of the roof showed that the three feet long stone balustrades were not tied down and consequently one gave way when it was leant upon. The Jury returned a verdict of accidental death, the affair being noted as most unfortunate and lamentable.

Crispins Arms

Elizabeth West was employed as a factory hand and lived at no 2 court D off Jewry Wall Street, she was often addled with drink spending long periods in the nearby Crispin's Arms. Concern for her youngest daughter had been voiced to the Prevention of Cruelty to Children society. In July 1892 the society's officer visited West to check on five month old Edith, the child was in a filthy condition, emaciated and very ill, Elizabeth was not at home but was soon found in the Crispin pub and cautioned over the treatment of her child.

A couple of weeks later the officer again visited West's home, the door was locked and she was again to be found in the Crispin's Arms worse for drink. She accompanied the officer back to her house where little Edith lay on a bed in a filthy old nightgown with a smelly and dirty under vest. She appeared in a worse condition than when least seen by the officer who sent for some milk, West then proceeded to feed the child from a spirit flask coated with congealed filth. Baby Edith drank the milk ravenously

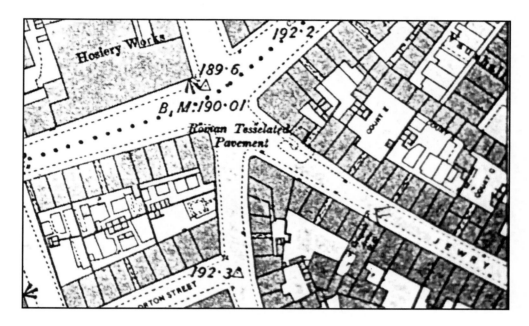

Crispin's Arms, Jewry Wall Street with the adjoining Courts

Two days later the officer called again, this time accompanied by Dr Peak, the baby was again found alone, with the mother in the Crispin's Arms, The Doctor took Edith away to the society's shelter in Friar Lane, where she was found to weigh under lbs. Baby Edith sadly died the next morning.

Eliza West 35 was charged with her manslaughter and wilful neglect of her child. At her trial, neighbours told of West visiting the pub two or three times a day sometimes for up too four hours at a time. After summing up his Lordship was minded to press for the manslaughter charge, but for the fact she had lost her child and she would have to live with that on her conscience also, she had five other children who needed her. After only five minutes the jury returned with a guilty verdict to the charge of wilful neglect. West was sentenced to only three weeks in gaol (a similar length of prison term would be given for poaching).

9
End of the line for the locals

Locals as we know them are disappearing at an alarming rate, Leicester has suffered as badly as any other city, many reasons are given, demographics, slum clearance, cultural changes etc. since the 1980s the acceleration of closures has been greater than any other period since the attempt in the early 1900's to rid the town of many of its 'undesirable' pubs under the Compensation Act. The ill-conceived Tory governments Beer Orders Act of 1990, restricted the amount of brewers owning retail public houses. This resulted in creating extremely large pub groups, more aptly described as property companies who had little other than an aim for bottom line profits from every outlet. Managers employed by the breweries largely disappeared and tenants replaced them often paying ever increasing rents and costs. Previously, brewers may have often let less profitable houses trade with small rents, as they owned the freehold and sold their beer, spirits and associated dry products, this helped to provide an overall profit on the balance sheet. Unfortunately the constant drive for profit prevailed and the premises were, and are still being sold off (many were in prime locations) for flats or other commercial developments.

Additionally much of Leicester's industry has declined dramatically over this period, hosiery companies such as T.W Kemptons, Wolsey and Corah's (Corah's at one time employed over 2,000 workers and British United Shoe Machinery, Leicester's largest employer, over 4,500) all have now closed and provided potential customers for a pint after work, a drink on a Friday lunchtime, a birthday, a retirement or leaving bash. The closure of these and so many other medium to large companies in the town had a huge effect on the nearby pubs.

Certainly a more discerning customer demands high quality service so poorly run outlets have always struggled. The Labour Governments idea of a café culture utopia meant major changes to the licensing system which resulted in more regulation and red tape forcing higher expenses for the publican. Additionally the handing out of licenses to any applicant with a shop (previously magistrates were accountable for this which worked well for 150 years), the politicians interference has meant no go areas for none but the brave aged over 25 on some evenings. Added to this is the smoking ban, health and safety, risk assessments, high utilities prices, publicans tied to large pub and property companies. All this has added to the price of a pint, so inevitably demand falls.

Beer at home means Davenports - well that's what the old advert used to say, now it means Tesco's or Sainsbury's where people can buy cheap booze and drink at home. Surely it can't replace the pub where the world can be put to rights over a chat, a pint and maybe if you are lucky really eye watering fun. If this sounds a little depressing and negative for the pub trade sorry it is.

There will also be success stories such as the Wetherspoons outlets providing cheap food and drink, and it may be said sometimes in the most ornate surroundings often creditably relative to the town or city in which they are sited. Hats off to them, sadly they too have contributed to the death of the small local. That is market forces at work it should be a kick up the backside for poorly run pubs, as always in any business only the fittest will survive!

Largely Lost, levelled, loved but not forgotten locals

Leicester has very few Pubs we would regard as old fashion locals, where little has changed over the years, among those lost through demolition or major alteration are;

The Bowlturners on Belgrave Gate. the 'Bollys' was one of the 'Holy Trinity' of 'Shippos' pubs together with the Brazier's on Russell Square and the Royal Oak, Belgrave Gate were true locals.

Hard to believe this photo of Bill & Ada was taken in 1993 in the bar of the 'Bollys', a couple of year's later a major refurbishment took place that knocked the heart from the Bowlturners.

Originally Shipstones of Nottingham would send the beer by train to the Great Northern station, in Belgrave Road, the dray horse would then deliver the beer to their pubs. Stables at the rear of the Bowlturners and one in Kent Street housed the Shire horses.

The Royal Oak in 1988 it was the first of the Shipstone's pubs in Leicester when the company took over Beeston Brewery in 1922. Originally it was two buildings the extension included the mortuary next door! Still standing

Busy, bustling and noisy, for decades the hub of the community, the Brazier's, Russell Square in 1994 boarded up and later demolished. Always known for its quality of the beer, like the other two, the 'craic' was evident throughout. Shipstone's owned more than a dozen pubs in Leicester most kept a super pint, a sad day when the brewery closed.

The Hat & Beaver, Highcross Street

This is one closure that could have been avoided, sitting on the edge of the new Shires, formally the Highcross shopping centre, it ceased to be a pub shortly before the centres opening.

A Georgian Inn that once brewed its own ale, previously owned by Brunt & Bucknell then Bass. They were forced to sell it off after the misconceived Tory government guidelines to the Monopolies & Mergers Commission. It fell into the hands of Hardy Hansons who until their takeover by Green King continued to trade at the Hat & Beaver. One of only a handful of pubs that stood on the same site with its name unchanged for over 200 years.

The Dominoes team at the 'Hat' can you spot the odd one out?

Hat & Beaver with its 'classic 1960's interior, a sad loss to Leicester's 'heritage pubs'

Make mine a pint of mild please Tony, anyone else want one?

Previous landlords, Ken and Jan labelled their cobs as meat or cheese, not ham, pork, beef or whatever just meat. You could have one and a pickled egg if you managed to avoid the pub's cat that often slept draped across the bar with its head nestling the beer pumps. Once when Jan was asked where Ken was that evening she replied he had gone *"up town"*, that's about twenty-five yards away! Jan was famous for her knitting, an ever constant flask of tea and bashing the tele' buttons with her window pole when any soap series dared to appear. A crude but effective early form remote control.

Only a handful of true 'locals' are left in Leicester that have survived major refits, it really doesn't take long to name them. Richard III, Highcross Street and the Black Horse Braunstone Gate are the only two to survive relatively intact, although both have undergone minor refits.

Followed behind these come a list that have retained some of their originality; Black Boy Albion Street, (now sadly closed) Cherry Tree Bond Street, Sir Charles Napier Glenfield Road, Pubs such as the Shakespeare Southgate Street (1960's rebuild but retains much of 60's fittings) Western-Western Road (still with its two rooms and bars). The Ale Wagon, Charles Street, ruined some 30 years ago but tastefully restored with original fittings which is commendable and finally the Globe Silver Street, with its front vaults surviving from the Victorian period. There may be the odd one left out, but that's about all Leicester can muster.

Of course there are many good pubs around, but retaining little of the original.

Richard III, still with some of its original Victorian features
coupled together with its 1960's fittings.

The ornate Victorian bar back that served the upstairs rooms at the Richard III.

Shakespeares Head , built in the 1960's much of the interior is original, if it survives
it might be looked upon in the future as a gem.

Did you know?

The Builders Arms, Erskine Street was the last of the beer only houses in the city to close
c 1974.

Since 1970 over 120 traditional pubs have closed in Leicester city. Many more have changed their
name, true lots of café-bars have come along to replace them, some good examples exist, but most
have had a short shelf life, passing through the history of Leicester's licensed premises without being
noticed. Below is a small snap shot of some of Leicester's lost taverns.

Watts, High Street affectionately known as Dr Watts. It was demolished for a new build called the Churchill in the 1960's. A grocery shop on one side of the entrance and a bar the other. In 1890 the company formally merged with Langmore and Bankart of All Saints' Brewery. This Victorian advert is from 1886.

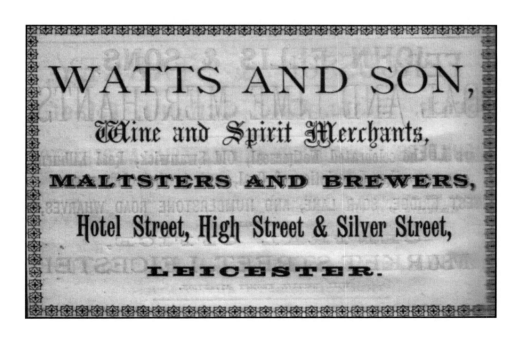

The White Swan, Market Place

Market Day, with the White Swan in the background, shortly before the old pub closed for demolition c 1974. Another old Leicester pub that evokes many memories for the cityite.

The Wine Lodge

Page's Wine Lodge

Dear Old Jetty, (or Jitty as we called it) wine lodge, also in the Market Place, only had a 6 day licence, no drink on a Sunday. A gem, a classic, enlarged and refurbished losing its uniqueness when taken over by Yates. Show business stars of the 40's & 50's such as Max Miller and Jimmy James would call in at the Jitty when appearing in Leicester. Wine, sherry and port attracted many of Leicester's older clientele. It was also popular with women who could hide away in one of the nooks and corners, the most charming of atmospheres and now sadly just another boozer.

Did you know?

That the Neptune c1850 (it became the West End and then Pump & Tap) had their toilets across the road in a French style 'pisseri' with a corrugated iron screen around, with the waste passing straight into the river.

The Magazine

The Magazine Newark Street, a local until its demise in 1999 it stood close to the old Town walls. On its demolition a roman burial ground was found underneath with 31 bodies in stone lined pots. The pub had a wide cross section of punters from students, arty types and some local characters. The old girl who ran the pub went out with a bang, whilst the demolition lads were having lunch she decided to do the work for them and the building collapsed into the street, happily no one was hurt, apart from the shock.

The Midland Arms, Fox Street.

Bob & Harry play 'devil among the tailors'

The pub was situated at the rear of the railway station, many of the railwaymen and postal workers used the Midland. Everards brewery closed it and transferred the licence to their new pub the Abbeydale in Wigston about 1963. The Leicester Mercury reported one regular on its closure remarking 'I've a good mind to give up drinking'

The Tavern

After the austere war years, pubs generally remained untouched, the coming of the late 50's and early 1960's saw a great change, and young people for the first time had money to spend, where to spend it? At the dance halls and pubs of course, jiving to the sounds of Little Richard, Eddie Cochrane, Chuck Berry etc at the Palais, Ill Rondo or Granby. Many of the surrounding pubs in the centre, were redesigned for the younger market usually with a trendier name change.

The Tavern in the Town, was refurbished for the young trade in the building that was previously occupied by the long time closed Black Lion on Belgrave Gate. The 'in the town' was dropped after the I.R.A. bombings of the pub of the same name in Birmingham. In the background can be seen a Younger's Tartan bitter sign, where underneath the new modern bar the Hollyrood stood.

The Old Black Lion

The Old Black Lion opposite the Palais became the Pickwick; this picture was taken after it had been renamed, but still retained its Black Lion emblem. Refurbished to attract the younger money with an artier name. It didn't last long only a few years; it later reverted to the Black Lion and is now called Scandals.

Did you know?

In 1955 the licensee of the De Montfort in Wellington Street was cautioned for permitting dancing in the lounge, when his music and singing licence only covered the bar!

The Haymarket Development

Tragically many fine old buildings were lost to accommodate the Haymarket shopping centre of the early 1970's, the following hotels and bars were demolished to make way for the planners drab concrete and red brick faceted eyesore.

Left; The Admiral Nelson with its Art Deco façade and its next door neighbour The Plough.

The Bell Hotel with its stylish Georgian façade.

The ornate Stag & Pheasant, originally Georgian it was rebuilt in 1905 and had a grillroom and champagne bar in between the wars. Many celebrities stayed there over the years including Gracie Fields and boxers such as Jack Dempsey and Larry Gains.

The Tower Vaults, Humberstone Gate, it stood next door to the Stag & Pheasant a couple of doors away from the Clock Tower.

The White Horse around the corner at 27 Belgrave Gate.

The fondly remembered Georgian White Hart with its mock Tudor façade.

A few doors down from the White Hart stood the 'Gothic' George.

The Star and Horse Repository, it was originally known as the Horse breakers.

Finally the Fleur de Lis, all eleven of these historic buildings were destroyed to make way for the Haymarket complex. After only 25 years it was looking so tired and run down it was planned to demolish large parts of it. However as a short-term solution it was given a makeover.

In contrast the city was treated to the following lovely new buildings of the Haymarket centre.

This section replaced the White Hart, note the lovely concrete balconies that are in such a dangerous and deteriorated state public access is no longer permitted.

This replaced the 'Gothic' George, note the symmetrical grain on the chipboard boarding up the widows and ....

The Alderman-Grange Lane

The Alderman was often referred to as the glass piano as the upright was surrounded by glass instead of wood. The Thomson family ran it for many years from the mid 1930s until the 1950s. The piano was a major talking point for the drinkers of Leicester.

The Alderman taken in the 1960s, it was a popular venue for the students at the nearby technical college, prior to finally closing about 1973.

A woolly hat day in The Alderman with the tea urn behind the bar, the lady at the back would probably prefer a stout or a barley wine

(photos by Tony Booker)

The pub stood on the corner of Humberstone gate and Gallowtree Gate the licensee was fined in 1919 under the deception order, for selling beer above the regularised prices, it closed in 1926 and was demolished for Burtons the Tailors to be built

Bucking the trend

A few pubs are bucking the trend, refurbishing back to near to the original as possible, most notably The Ale Wagon in Charles Street and The Western in Western Road.

Credit must go to the Hoskins family for their efforts to return as close as possible to its original format.

The Western with its intact Victorian facade and internal refurbishment.

The 1930's Ale Wagon, one of Leicester's few remaining 'local boozers'

The Mitre and Keys

The Mitre and Keys on Applegate Street stood opposite the Holiday Inn close to the entrance of Castle Street. It was one of Leicester's ancient inns and had a tunnel connecting it to the Castle; it was rebuilt in the 1890s

The rear of The Mitre and Keys, by the Leicester artist John Flower (1793-1861), first printed in 1826.

The Mitre and Keys was one of many pubs to go in the reconstruction of the area in the 1960s, the Holiday Inn development saw a large scale destruction of ancient streets, Applegate Street, Redcross Street and Harvey's Lane to name but a few, they often totally disappeared.. Today the Holiday Inn is a classic example of what Prince Charles may describe as '*an architectural carbuncle*'.

After its closure in 1959, (its licence was later transferred to The Rowlett at Rowlett's Hill, which opened in 1971) the old Mitre and Keys pub was used for a time as a youth centre,

Barry Lount has fond memories of the youth centre;

'*I remember the centre very well it was open long after other places had closed for the evening. We knew it as Rays after Ray Gosling who was the young guy who ran it. He was of a similar age, dressed in the same fashion and was seen more as a 'mate' rather than a figure of authority. It was informal, you could just drop in whenever you liked, for its day it was quite radical – ahead of the time.*

The centre was backed by a charity called Youth Venture, (something I did not find out until after it had closed), supported by a number of celebrities and well known people including Tommy Steele, who was a well known singer and performer of the time. The intention was that they would open a number of these venues across the country. Sadly the informality proved to be part of its downfall and the centre was closed after reoccurring trouble and numerous fights.

Ray Gosling then went on to become a successful writer and presenter on television, which included documentaries on Leicester and the East Midlands'.

Dedications

To my father, who was brought up in a Leicester pub, and to my mother both
of whose families showed me more love than I deserved. I never fully realised
the hardship of their upbringing.

Barry Lount 2012

For Victoria and James, sometimes when I write I make myself cry, mostly through laughter.
When I don't cry anymore I know it will be time to stop writing.

Robert Spurr 2012

Acknowledgements

Research was conducted at the Leicester Records Office and Leicester Reference Libraries (now the Central Library) covering many varied sources of information, and our thanks go to their staff. Help was also given by Newark Houses Museum. Leicester City Planning Office, Steve England at the Leicester Mercury. Everards Brewery, Chris Pyrah, Joseph Regan and Les Pateman's lists and records. Sid Savage, Pollard's drayman, a workmate who ferried Barry around Leicester's pubs in the late 1950's, a true gentleman. The Hoskins family at the Ale Wagon for their hospitality and insults.

Photos are mainly from Barry's collection but thanks go to John Zientek, John Manners, Mick and Marion(Ex Bollys), Paddy McCracken and Tony Booker for the loan of their photos, stories and anecdotes from Ray Turner, Geoff Blackburn, Mo Brandon, George & Vera Rudkin, Tom & Charlie Hargrave and Aunt Jean, Apologies to those who gave stories, who's names we wrote down but couldn't find them the next morning. Baz Deacon and Karen Hobson for photo's, moral support and practical research, visiting the many beer emporiums. And especially Chris Jinks who has an encyclopaedic knowledge on Leicester pubs.

Elizabeth Roff for her many hours with her red pen and scissors, proof reading, correcting and amending our work.

Finally we would like to thank the people of Leicester, undoubtedly the largest contributors and without them this could never have been written.

Bibliography

Radical Leicester. A. Temple Patterson University College Leicester 1954.

Poverty and the Workhouse in Victorian Britain. Peter Wood, Sutton Publishing Stroud Gloucestershire 1991.

Records of the Borough of Leicester volumes 5,6, and 7 G.A. Chinnery Leicester University Press from 1965 –1974.

St Marks Church Leicester Victorian Society

Leicester the Ancient Borough. 1983 Jack Simmons, Alan Sutton Publishing, Brunswick Road, Gloucester.

The Condition of the Working Class in England. Fredrick Engles, Granada Publishing Limited, St Albans, Herts. 1969.

The Cradle and Home of the Hosiery Trade by A. J. Pickering, published by F. Pickering 1940.

History of Machine-Wrought Hosiery Manufacture by W. Felkin first published in 1867.

Minutes of Evidence Taken Before the Commission for Inquiring into the Condition of the Framework Knitter, Published in 1845.

In Sickness and in Health by Clive Harrison published by Leicester City Council 1999.

Working-Class Life in Victorian Leicester, The Joseph Dare Reports. By Barry Haynes published by Leicestershire Libraries and Information Service 1991.

Leicestershire's Lunatics by Henry Orme and William Orme published by Leicestershire Museums Publications 1987.

St Margaret's select Vestry- its history and work by Ernest Morris, undated.

The Workhouse, Norman Longhmate published by Pimlico 2003.

The English Poor in the Eighteenth Century by Dorothy Marshall published by Rutledge & Kegan Paul Ltd 1969.

William Bradley, The Yorkshire Giant, Keith Lowe, Market Weighton Chamber of Trade un-dated.

Leicestershire County Cricket Club, by Dennis Lambert, Tempus Publishing Limited, 2000.

Old Leicester, by David Clarke and Jack Simmons, the Leicestershire Archaeological and Historical Society, 1962.

The True History of the Elephant Man, M Howell & P. Ford, published by Allison & Busby 1980.

Pigot's Commercial Directory 1828.

White's, Kelly's and Wright's Directories 1848 – 1968.

Weston's Directory 1794

A history of the County of Leicester volume 4, Oxford University Press 1958.

Fowler's Directory 1815.

Drake and Melville's directories.

The Times Newspaper Archive.

Census returns 1841-1901

The Leicester Royal Infirmary 1771-1971 E. Frizelle & J Martin, published by Leicester No 1 Hospital Management Company 1971.

Leicester Family History Society Marriage Indices.

Records of the Borough of Leicester volumes 1-4 edited by Mary Bateson and Helen Stocks Cambridge University Press, 1901

Narrow Boat, L.T.C. Rolt, Eyre & Spottswood, 1944.

History in Leicester, Colin Ellis, City of Leicester Publicity Depatment Information Bureau, 1948

Radical Leicester, A Temple Patterson, University College Leicester 1954.

The Leicestershire Historian volume one onwards from 1967, extracts from various contributors.

Community History Newsletter, various contributors, extracts, Community History, Central Learning and Information Library Bishop Street.

Leicester Past and Present, Jack Smmons, Eyre Methuen, 1974.

Leicester Civic, Industrial and Social Life 1927, compiled by Charles Howes, The Midland Services Agencies Ltd. 1927.

William Gardiner, Johnathon Wiltshire 1970, published by Leicester Research Services.

Glimpses of Ancient Leicester (revised edition 1906) Mrs A. Fielding Johnson.

Old and New London - Edward Walford 1878.

Royal Progresses and visits to Leicester, W Nelly 1884.

Sketches and Caricatures - Alehouses of Oadby, Punch, midland Jackdaw, Town Crier. Connent Collection, David Buttery, George Davenport, Leicester Notorious Highwaymen.

Meet the authors

Barry, a war baby, grew up in Oadby, having 'successfully' failed to pass the 11 plus, he was educated at Gartree school.

He aspired to become a chef but a Youth Employment Officer sent him to learn the drinks trade at Pollards Brewery in Leicester, where he attained the lofty position of a Lorry Driver's mate. Visiting the pubs in and around Leicester during the late 1950's gave him an insight into another world and a chance to meet many of Leicester's characters, which resulted in a life-time's interest in social and local history.

Barry has written history books concerning Leicester alehouses, highwayman George Davenport, and James Hawker a Victorian Poacher. A licensee for most of his working life, he founded the Steamin' Billy Brewing Company which has several public houses in and around Leicester.

He married Liz in his teens and has two daughters and two grandchildren. He is a proud Leicester lad who supports Leicester City, the Tigers and the Leicestershire cricket team.

Robert was born at home in Leicester. He attended Coleman Road infant school before successfully reaching the age to graduate to the junior school. He first met Barry nearly 20 years ago, somewhat surprisingly in a local pub.

He has written many articles largely concerning local social history and finds the often newly re discovered subjects fascinating, sometimes tragic but often extremely funny.

His ambition is to buy a young parrot, teach it to swear loudly and continually then leave it to a 'favourite' person in his will. Please be warned, as he has not yet decided on that special person-it could be you.

Robert has two children, one grandson, and a parrot on order.